05/07

KU-525-820

The transformation
of the year one thousand
The village of Lournand
from antiquity to feudalism

GUY BOIS
translated by Jean Birrell

Manchester University Press
Manchester and New York

distributed exclusively in the USA by Palgrave

First published in French as *La Mutation de l'an Mil* by
Librairie Arthème Fayard, © 1989

Published by Manchester University Press
Oxford Road, Manchester M13 9NR, UK
and Room 400, 175 Fifth Avenue, New York, NY 10010, USA

Distributed exclusively in the USA by
Palgrave, 175 Fifth Avenue, New York,
NY 10010, USA

Distributed exclusively in Canada by
UBC Press, University of British Columbia, 2029 West Mall,
Vancouver, BC, Canada V6T 1Z2

British Library Cataloguing-in-Publication Data
A catalogue record for this book is available
from the British Library

Library of Congress-Cataloging-in-Publication Data
Bois, Guy.
    [Mutation de l'an mil. English]
    The transformation of the year one thousand: the village of
    Lournand from antiquity to feudalism / Guy Bois : translated
    by Jean Birrell.
        p.   cm.
    Translation of: La mutation de l'an mil.
    Includes index.
    ISBN 0–7190–3565–1. — ISBN 0–7190–3566–X (pbk.)
    1. France—Social conditions—To 987—Case studies.
    2. France—Social conditions—987–1515—Case studies.
    3. Lournand (France)—Social conditions—Case studies.
    4. Feudalism—France—Case Studies.   5. Peasantry—France—
    History—Case studies.   I. Title.   HN425.B6313   1992
    306'.0944—dc20   92–1488

ISBN 0 7190 3565 1 *hardback*
       0 7190 3566 X *paperback*

Reprinted in paperback 1997, 2000, 2002

Typeset in Galliard
by Northern Phototypesetting Co. Ltd., Bolton
Printed in Great Britain
by Bell & Bain Limited, Glasgow

Contents

Plates

The plates appear between pages 134 and 135

Abbreviations

A. C. de Cluny	Archives communales de Cluny
Annales-ESC	Annales: Economies, Sociétés, Civilisations
C. C.	Recueil des chartes de l'abbaye de Cluny

Preface

From time to time, I long to reopen the *Recueil des Chartes de Cluny* and return to work. Forty years on, the study of eleventh- and twelfth-century society in the Mâconnais with which I made my debut as a historian is in need of revision, correction, even completion; its imperfections strike me whenever I chance to reread a few pages. I could take advantage both of the revisions which constantly revitalise historical research and of the progress in that very field which I chose to explore. The rigorous treatment of these documents by the medievalists of Münster would make it possible to identify more places and people, and so improve the dating, reconstruct denser networks of relationships and trace more accurately the fortunes of lineages and patrimonies.

Now, Guy Bois has anticipated me. Almost by chance; he has been spending his summers at Lournand, near Cluny, that is at the very heart of the little territory which is perhaps best documented in the whole of the West for the late tenth and early eleventh centuries, a crucial period here, furthermore, since a brutal rupture then pre-cipitated the evolution of social relations. Quite naturally, Guy Bois, in his turn, decided to exploit this documentary wealth. Con-centrating on a different period, examining older texts, very different structures and unsatisfactory interpretations, he poses similar ques-tions to those he recently so magisterially answered in his distin-guished study of fifteenth-century Normandy. This time, he starts from the bottom, from the narrowest of bases, that is from one village and its environs, but he proceeds to increasingly broad perspectives. In the end, he has written a work of general history. It is a major study. It is also an encouraging one.

There has been some unease that French historians, given the collapse of ideology, might no longer tackle large projects, that their work might continue to fragment, and degenerate into 'petite histoire'. Reading this book, one is reassured. Rejecting nothing and free from all constraints, adding what is newest in the work of

Fernand Braudel to conceptual tools borrowed from Marxism, though first cleaned, honed and polished, paying equal attention to all the 'instances', whether they derive from the material or the non-material, as interested in religion as in demography or techniques of production, fully aware of the discordances between the various strands which interconnect within one same process, Guy Bois has constructed a model. He has done so carefully, clearly and cautiously. He has dared to propose a global, entirely new and coherent explanation of a transition, or rather of a revolution. He has proposed a theory of the transition which substituted for the 'ancient' social system that other system which we continue to call 'feudal'.

It is a bold, an attractive and a provocative essay. It is disturbing; it calls for historians to delve deeper, to follow up leads, to compare, to examine events elsewhere, not only at the same time but earlier and later, to verify, and to criticise. And criticised this book will be, perhaps in part demolished, but therein lies its value. It will stimulate research, raising once again a hundred dormant questions. For example, is it correct to attribute such a leading role here, in the year 1000, to the small estate and the free peasantry? Should one not, first, look more carefully at the interior of that enormous organism so close by, the abbey of Cluny? Would it not be helpful, using all the means by which we can today identify filiations and marriage alliances more reliably, to examine for a wider area the structures of the ruling class, the strata which composed it, the antagonisms which divided it, and the solidarities which gave it its strength? Was the relationship between feudalisation and the opening up of the market so simple? Would one not obtain a clearer picture by extending the investigation over a longer period, beyond the documentary lacuna of the twelfth century, to find material of an equivalent abundance and richness, with which one could compare? Questions arise on all sides, and new possibilities of research open up in a field one might have thought exhausted.

The work which issues this salutary challenge is, however, solidly and firmly constructed. It is an impressive achievement, lucid and harmonious, and it will not easily be demolished. Guy Bois is persuasive, and able to communicate his own enthusiasm. I have said that he has anticipated me; far from having dampened my desire to return to my old documents, he has made it seem more pressing.

Georges Duby
Académie française

Introduction

This book is unusual in a way the reader should be aware of from the outset. The events it describes took place not only in an obscure village, but in a period which is among the most mysterious in our history. The tenth century has left few traces in our collective memory. The great figures of the Carolingian dynasty, Pepin the Short, Charlemagne and Louis the Pious, are long gone. After them came only pale shadows, whose names have never cluttered the pages of scholarly manuals, and who soon retreated before a new dynasty established by Hugh Capet (987). When we remember how little historians know even about this king, we may begin to appreciate the depths of the period's obscurity.

Why, then this book? Not to be sure, from any taste for paradox. The enterprise is worthwhile for two simple reasons. Firstly, because the tenth century preceded the birth of feudal society. It was a time of gestation, perhaps even of final contractions, and for this reason it is of particular interest; to observe the birth of a society is perhaps the best way to understand it. Consequently, no effort should be spared which might throw light on such a decisive moment. The second reason derives from a happy conjunction of circumstances. We are, by luck or by accident, exceptionally well informed about this almost unknown village, dignified by no remarkable event, distinguished by no special features. We are able to penetrate deep into it, and know its inhabitants one by one, by name, status, place of residence and activities. We are, in fact, in the presence of a tiny island of light in a sea of darkness. Such an opportunity must be seized. This will not, it should be stressed, be merely the history of one village for its own sake. It is of interest to us only as an exemplar of the social fabric of the period. Let me make this clear: my book is intended as a piece of general history, and my main aim is to achieve a better understanding of the transformation which took place around the year 1000. It is only secondarily a monograph; as such it serves only to illumine a more general discussion.

Some unanswered questions

The discussion will, of course, be rooted in questions of special concern to its author. In this it is inseparable from a discussion of the present condition of medieval history.

Let us not paint too gloomy a picture. In the last fifty years, since the publication of Marc Bloch's *Caractères originaux de l'histoire rurale française*,[1] the point of departure for a profound historical revival, the discipline has undoubtedly made remarkable progress. Its methods have been renewed and its perspectives enlarged. Our knowledge of the societies called 'medieval' has been the chief beneficiary.

But we should not, for all that, lose sight of the other side of the coin. Many questions remain unanswered. I refer here not to any one particular aspect, rather to questions which are central to the history of every society, but which, regrettably, are often obscured by a too narrow scholarship (this is the case with everything concerning the dynamic, and even the identity, of these societies). For example, what do we know about the famous medieval growth? Everyone is agreed that it was important. It propelled Europe on to the forefront of the world stage (on the technical, economic and intellectual plane) well before the Renaissance and the discovery of the New Worlds. But what do we know about its chronology? Did it take off in the eleventh century or in the Frankish period? What were the profound mainsprings of this growth? The habitual (and lamentable) recourse to explanations of a demographic character is the best illustration of our failure – as if an excess of births over deaths in itself sufficed to launch a society on the road to development. It is the same with another, and closely connected, issue, that is the spectacular reversal of urban history. Only its chronology is clear – first a long process of de-urbanisation (or, if preferred, of ruralisation) beginning in the Late Empire, then, from the end of the tenth century, a process of urbanisation which transformed medieval society to make of it the progenitor of the modern world. Have we a satisfactory explanation for so decisive an event in the general history of Europe?

To these questions of historical dynamic are added others, even more troublesome, relating to the identity if medieval societies. It is essential to recognise that we are still employing conceptual tools which are five centuries old; the notion of the Middle Ages is a product of the Renaissance. That it is still in use and serves as the framework for the teaching of history at all levels is an aberration whose harmful consequences it is impossible to exaggerate, since it confers a fictitious unity on the period between the decline of the Roman Empire and the great discoveries. It implies the existence of a 'medieval' or 'feudal' society whose principal features were fixed at an early date, soon after the migrations of the Germanic peoples. Are we really sure this is so? The corollary, what is more, is a singularly vague characterisation of the society so designated: political fragmentation, a landowning aristocracy, a strong and vital Christianity. Does this definition identify what was the essence? That these frameworks of thought and research are increasingly obsolete and decreasingly serviceable is shown by the proliferation of cracks appearing in the façade of the old edifice. When, for example, Georges Duby advanced the hypothesis of a 'feudal revolution' around the year 1000, he was questioning, at least implicitly, the unity of the medieval period.[2] So was Pierre Bonnassie when he demonstrated the persistence of slavery throughout the Frankish period. Others have (wisely) renounced the term 'High Middle Ages' to indicate the fifth to tenth centuries, preferring 'Late Antiquity'.[3]

Most of all, it needs to be appreciated that criticism of the traditional schema is neither a theological quarrel nor a formalistic debate which boils down to a question of names. It concerns essential issues of historical research. As soon as the birth of the Middle Ages is made to follow immediately on the invasions, the process of the birth of the new society is obscured, even conjured away; the emphasis is put on the fusion between victors and vanquished, on their respective contributions in the fields of institutions, religion and the economy. The social change, consequently perceived as the result of ethno-cultural influences, is diluted over the long term. A simple reality is then lost from view; every human society is based on a set of structures which give its functioning a coherence and a rigidity which are incompatible with a scarcely perceptible transition from one type of functioning to another. That ancient and feudal societies reposed on radically different principles, and that the transition from one to the other could not in consequence be a minor matter, is equally ignored. Other historical examples, such as the future emergence of capitalism within the heart of the feudal system, surely show the length and the complexity of the processes by which a change of society is brought about. Old societies are a long time a-dying; even as their sap drains away, they remain upright, and their spreading roots obstruct the growth of new shoots. These processes of confrontation need to be examined with care, since they are the best indicators of the identity of the old and the new. If we wish to understand the nature of feudal society, we need first to understand its birth.

Without further prolonging these observations of a general nature, which will be developed later, let us at this stage simply note three points. Firstly, the problematic adopted here represents a radical break with the 'dominant' problematic(s). It is opposed not to any particular conception but to a general approach and its basic concepts. Rejecting the notion of the 'Middle Ages', it does not see the notion of 'feudal society' as a sort of scientific given, but as a subject which remains to be identified. Lastly, it aims to link the problems of social dynamic mentioned above to this attempt at identification.

Secondly, the investigation will be primarily organised around the birth of feudal society, in the hope that an examination of this process will throw light on the structures of that society. The projector has therefore deliberately been turned on the tenth century, to place us on the eve of decisive transformations whose import and significance we need to appreciate.

Lastly, the method chosen is that of micro-history. Since the aim is to diagnose the condition of a social fabric, it is essential to probe as deeply as possible and, consequently, ruthlessly narrow down the field of observation. In fact, the historian is faced with the same demands as the biologist or the physicist; the infinitely tiny or the elementary cell become ever more indispensable to his analysis. If essential changes occurred between the ancient and the feudal periods, it is surely at the level of the village itself that they should first be sought.

Why Lournand?

The choice of Lournand was dictated by the conjunction of three favourable circumstances. The first is a question of documentation. The principal obstacle for the historian of these remote periods is, as can easily be imagined, the paucity of the available sources. Abundant after 1300 (thanks to the progress of institutions and culture), they are rare for the preceding centuries and frankly exiguous prior to the year 1000. The retreat of writing in social life was such that only a limited number of texts emanating from the public authority or ecclesiastical institutions, especially monastic, have survived. The investigation to be undertaken was thus inconceivable on a general plane: it could only be attempted for a village which offered, thanks to special circumstances – in this case, the foundation of the abbey of Cluny – good conditions of observation, that is abundant sources of high quality.

In Lournand, we have at our disposal for the tenth century an observatory which is exceptional (Mediterranean regions such as Catalonia and Latium apart). In 909 or 910, a small community of monks under the direction of Abbot Berno settled four kilometres away, on the initiative of William, surnamed the Pious, duke of Aquitaine and count of Mâcon.[4] They were endowed with a collection of lands and property corresponding roughly to the territory of Cluny. Very soon, inspired by an ambitious project for monastic reform, this community extended its influence and endeavoured to increase its landed patrimony by acquisitions and, above all, by attracting donations from laymen who were affected by the ardour of its social message (denunciation of the wealth of the powerful and a clearly expressed desire to bring succour to the poor).

This explains the compilation of a very large number of deeds, comparable to contemporary notarials deeds, ratifying the various land transactions concluded with landowners in the vicinity. Each one is usually precisely dated, and gives the name of the donor or donors (or vendors), and nature of the property concerned (field, meadow, vineyard etc.), and very often its area and more or less precise location, with reference to its 'confines' (that is the names of those in possession of the neighbouring parcels). The vast majority of these deeds to have survived were edited in the last century, thanks to the labours of Alexander Bruel, with the title *Recueil des chartes de l'abbaye de Cluny*, in six large volumes.[5] They are a mine of information about the rural landscape as well as the economy and society of the Cluny region. This incomparable source has fascinated generations of historians. The list of works based on it is long. André Deléage, one of the ablest disciples of Marc Bloch, studied the cartulary of Cluny with great care and intelligence.[6] A little later, Georges Duby in his turn used these texts for *La Société aux XIe et XIIe siècles dans la région mâconnaise*, his epoch-making doctoral thesis.[7] Many others deserve mention here.[8] The soil, in fact, far from being virgin, has been repeatedly ploughed. These works have greatly assisted my own research.

We have therefore a documentation without parallel for tenth-century France. Further, Lournand, close to Cluny and soon to become one of the favoured territories of the monks (in the twelfth century, it was the abbey's first granary), is one of the two or three villages for which the deeds are most numerous. It is thus not unreasonable to see it as the village which offers the best conditions of study for the tenth century, in general so obscure.

The second reason for the choice of Lournand derives from its representativeness. This is equally important, for reasons which need to be spelled out. Lournand was, in effect, an entirely typical village of that period, that is, it was situated at some distance from an urban centre. The town, in this case, was Mâcon (the town of Cluny did not yet exist), about thirty kilometres away, where both count and bishop resided. This was the most common situation, I repeat, since the urban network had not yet been modified by the dissemination of the little *bourgs* so characteristic of the feudal era; it retained the wider mesh of the gallo-Roman urban network of which it was the distant heir.

It is necessary to emphasise this point because most of what we know, or think we know, about Carolingian society concerns precisely those rural communities which were not in this common situation. Our information is largely based on those documents familiar to every student of history called polyptychs, inventories of great lay or ecclesiastical estates. They describe vast units of exploitation, of several hundred hectares, or even larger, divided into two elements: a 'demesne' exploited for the benefit of the owner, and lands committed to tenants (some free, others considered to be unfree) in return for rents and labour services performed on the demesne. An immense historical literature has been based on the polyptychs;[9] a list of works devoted to them over the last five years alone would in itself take up entire pages. Miracles of ingenuity have been performed to expose their pitfalls and exploit their strengths. This is perhaps hardly surprising when one remembers how little else there is into which historians can sink their teeth.

The result has been an almost classic representation of the Carolingian world from the economic and social standpoint. It is to be found in all textbooks of history, and is still the basis for what students are taught. At its heart lies the manorial system or mode of exploitation employed on the 'great estates', characterised by the organic link established between demesne and tenures (or 'manses') by the labour rent of the tenants. On the social plane, the free and the unfree lived side by side on the tenures, and the difference between their respective statuses was diminishing, which suggests that slavery had disappeared or was on the point of disappearing. The great estate has been taken as the basic molecule of the social system, only one step away from the seigneurial system. Social power derived from possession of land, so that the large landowner was inexorably transformed into a veritable seigneur possessing powers of constraint over his tenants. This has given substance to the notion of the society of the High Middle Ages as being already highly feudalised, and justified the traditional view of the Middle Ages referred to above.

The problem does not lie in the validity of the conclusions based on the study of the polyptychs, which are, in fact, of great interest. It lies in the central role incautiously attributed to the manorial system and the social structures associated with it. For twenty years, a revision has been under way. Firstly, it became apparent through various regional studies (including that of Robert Fossier on Picardy)[10] that there existed an important sector of small peasant landownership which completely escaped the structures of the manorial system; it had hitherto been almost entirely unknown, since the humble always leave less written evidence of their presence than the powerful. But the severest blow to the old schemas came from a Belgian historian of exceptional rigour, Adriaan Verhulst.[11] Quite simply, he showed that the great Carolingian estate, far from having been the rule, was the exception. It emerged in very special circumstances, around Paris, in the shadow of Frankish power, by an act of voluntarism made possible by the proximity of royal power. That it should be found here and there elsewhere, associated with great monasteries invested with public power, is hardly surprising but not enough to justify assuming its wide diffusion.

There has thus begun, if slowly, a fundamental revision of the place of the great estate and an acceptance that it should no longer be seen as a dominant structure. It is arguable, however, whether the consequences of Verhulst's discovery have been fully appreciated. The assertions generally made as regards the evolution of the servile condition or the respective roles of servitude and freedom are based on sources which relate, we now realise, to exceptional situations. We should perhaps cease to base on them conclusions of general application.

The principal interest of the example of Lournand for the study of economic and social structures is that it enables us to escape from these exceptional situations and approach the normality of the tenth century. As soon, in fact, as we move eight or ten kilometres away from Mâcon, the comital or episcopal estates lose all their stability and the public power is exercised less firmly. If a typical structure existed, this is surely where we should seek it.

Such considerations are not sufficient, of course, on which to base claims as to the typicality of our example (nor do we claim to erect Lournand into a model). From the north to the south of the old Gaul, rural civilisation presents too many diversities of geographical or historical origin not to render any generalisation imprudent. Let us note only that Lournand is situated a few kilometres to the south of the great linguistic, juridical and technical frontier separating northern from southern France. The village thus lies at the point of contact of the two main agrarian zones. It lies within a 'pays', the Mâconnais, of precocious agricultural development. Prehistory is here present at every step. The Gauls settled in large numbers and are probably responsible for the remarkable 'civilisation of hamlets' discussed by André Deléage, which is also found in Auvergne and well beyond, throughout central France. Then came Rome, and with it a dense scatter of *villae*, exploitations of truly colonial type, an indelible trace of which is to be found on our territory, in the hamlet of Collonge. There were also Germanic settlers (Burgundians and, above all, Franks) close by, on the other side of the River Grosne, in the hamlet of Varanges. All the classical ingredients of the future feudal society are to be found here.

In sum, we are dealing with an illustration of central France; or more precisely, a little grouping at its heart, situated near to the great southern route of penetration (the Saône–Rhone axis), and enjoying, thanks to its gently sloping limestone hillsides, soils which were easy to cultivate. For these two reasons, the exploitation of the soil and the density of population both achieved high levels at a very early date, by antiquity; this is a singularity which to some extent restricts the significance of the example and which should be borne firmly in mind.

The third reason for the choice of Lournand will appear more clearly at the end of this book. It derives from the role played by Cluny in the feudal transformation or revolution. The monks were its principal protagonists, on the level of both theory and action. The Cluny region was, as a result, in the centre of the storm, and the village of Lournand itself was directly involved in these events. As a result, it is not without interest to look more closely at the local social realities which Abbots Maïeul and Odilo, and also their predecessors, confronted; as also at the reactions of the various elements in village society to the activities encouraged by the monastery. We may perhaps discover here some enlightenment as to the significance of the upheavals surrounding the year 1000.

The observatory

We need next to describe the surroundings in which the events took place, and note the essential reference points. We are dealing with a small hilly area on either side of the Grosne, which runs from south to north at the bottom of a flat valley, some 500 to 700 metres wide, and at an altitude of about 240 metres. Two ridges of high ground, oriented north/south, bound this unit. To the west are densely wooded sandstone hills, culminating in la Denturgue (nearly 500 metres), which adjoins the neighbouring Charolais. To the east, a crest between 500 and 600 metres high separates our region from the interior of the Mâconnais. The modern commune of Lournand occupies the western part of this territory. It has some level ground, but consists mostly of hills, slopes and small valleys. The *bourg* of Lournand (a Gallic place-name meaning 'the little valley of Lur', a Gallic personal name) is situated in the most pronounced of the small valleys, separated from Cluny to the south by the stony uplands of the Crâ, dominated to the north by a spur crowned with the ruins of the castle of Lourdon (which belonged to the abbey after having been one of the principal fortresses of the *pagus* or county of Mâcon and probably previously a Gallic *oppidum*).

Apart from the *bourg*, the population of the commune is distributed between several hamlets, of which the largest, Collonge, to the north, enjoys the best agricultural land and gives the area its very characteristic twin-peaked appearance. Smaller, but also endowed with its own personality, Chevagny, situated in a little valley, forms a sort of buffer-hamlet squeezed between the other two. There are two other centres of population which, as we will see, always existed within the orbit of the *bourg* of Lournand: Sous-Lourdon, huddled at the foot of the castle, and La Chaume, on the high ground (390 metres) to the west. There are also several outlying settlements which will be mentioned later. To give some impression, according to the departmental statistics of 1824, the 1,150 hectares of the cadastral area consisted of 22.4 per cent woodland, 49.5 per cent arable, 10.7 per cent vines and 9.9 per cent meadow.

However, by fixing the communal boundary on the River Grosne, the Revolution introduced an artificial barrier which we must cross. The hamlets of Merzé and Cotte were closely associated with Lournand. Of the latter there survives only one farm, situated in the ancient church; Merzé has retained its mill and a few houses. Both are in the valley, hemmed in to the east by a terrace of heavy soils and infertile deposits, most of which is still wooded. We need to go further east still to find, with the outcrops of Jurassic limestone, a landscape comparable to that between Lournand and Collonge, with arable and vines. The settlement here, perceptibly more concentrated, is divided between two principal agglomerations, Varanges and Cortambert.

Although we will be concentrating on Lournand and Collonge with their hamlets of Cotte and Merzé, reference will often be made to Varanges and Cortambert, since this little geographical unit corresponded in the tenth century to a judicial circumscription, probably ancient but its origins obscure, called the *ager* of Merzé.[12] This was the first level of the public institutions, constituted by the assembly of the '*francs*', that is the men of free status. Also, the richest landowners, for whom we will later use the term 'masters' or 'large allod-holders', usually held land on both sides of the Grosne, sometimes even further afield.

Such is our chosen area, not, in practice, very different from that we see today. The distribution of the population between the network of hamlets and dependencies has changed very little over a thousand years, apart from the decline of the two valley settlements (Merzé and Cotte), begun during the great crisis of the end of the Middle Ages and completed by the politico-religious conflicts of the second half of the sixteenth century. The agrarian landscape has shown a similar stability; even the low dry stone walls bounding the numerous parcels can be traced in the acts recording land transactions. The only significant modifications are recent; they consist of the retreat of the vine and arable in favour of grass, and the consequences – in any case limited – of rural regrouping.

We need now to enter without further delay the village of Lournand as it appears in the documents of the tenth century, principally, that is, on the basis of the cartulary of Cluny. If this were a local monograph, an analytical presentation would be required: a description in turn of the land, the people, society, production, the organisation of power. But my prime purpose, I repeat, is to try to answer certain questions of general application. The structure of my book is the direct expression of this concern. It is based on an examination of the five issues I regard as crucial for an understanding of the situation in the tenth century and its subsequent transformation: the role of slavery; the social structure taken globally; town/country relations and the role of trade; agrarian growth during the Frankish period; and, lastly, the political, social and ideological revolution of the end of the century.

Notes

1 Marc Bloch, *Les Caractères originaux de l'histoire rurale française*, Paris, 1931 (translated by Janet Sondheimer as *French Rural History*, London, 1966).

2 Georges Duby, *Les Trois Ordres ou l'imaginaire du féodalisme*, Paris, 1978, pp. 183ff. (translated by Arthur Goldhammer as *The Three Orders. Feudal Society Imagined*, Chicago and London, 1980).

3 Pierre Bonnassie, 'Survie et extinction du régime esclavagiste dans l'Occident du haut Moyen Age (IVe–XIe siècles)', *Cahiers de civilisation médiévale*, XXVIII, 1985, pp. 307–43 (translated by Jean Birrell as 'The survival and extinction of the slave system in the early medieval West' in P. Bonnassie, *From Slavery to Feudalism in South-Western Europe*, Cambridge, 1991).

4 For the history of the abbey of Cluny, see the recent synthesis of Marcel Pacaut, *L'Ordre de Cluny (909–1789)*, Paris, 1986.

5 *Recueil des chartes de l'abbaye de Cluny* ed. A. Bruel, 6 volumes, Paris, 1876–1903.

6 André Deléage, *La Vie rurale en Bourgogne jusqu'au début du XIe siècle*, 3 volumes, Mâcon, 1942.

7 Georges Duby, *La Société aux XIe et XIIe siècles dans la région mâconnaise*, Paris, first published 1953, re-ed. 1982.

8 Notably the many works of Maurice Chaume, including *Les Origines du duché de Bourgogne*, 4 volumes, Dijon, 1925–43; also, N. P. Gracianskij, *Burgundskaja derevnja u X–XII stoletjah*, Moscow, 1935.

9 See the recent bibiliography and discussion by Yosiki Morimoto, 'Etat et perspectives des recherches sur les polyptiques carolingiens', *Annales de l'Est*, II, 1988; also A. Verhulst, *Le Grand Domaine aux époques mérovingienne et carolingienne*, Ghent, 1985.

10 Robert Fossier, *La Terre et les hommes en Picardie jusqu'à la fin du XIIe siècle*, Paris–Louvain, 1968.

11 A. Verhulst, 'La genèse du régime domanial classique en France au haut Moyen

Age', *Agricoltura e mondo rurale in Occidente nell'alto medioevo, Settimane*, XIII, 1966, pp. 135–60.

12 On the significance of the *ager*, see the discussion by F. Bange, 'L'*ager* et la *villa*: structures du paysage et du peuplement dans la région mâconnaise à la fin du haut Moyen Age (XIe–IXe siècle)', *Annales-ESC*, 1984, pp. 529–69.

1
A slave society

Our first foray into the cartulary of Cluny will be exclusively devoted to labour. Every society is, in fact, primarily defined by the way in which its productive activities are organised, on the real as on the imaginary plane. Who does what and for whose benefit? How is labour perceived and how does this perception fit into a global system of values (in other words, ideology)?

The answer appears, at first sight, to be simple. The population of Lournand was for the most part composed of men and women who worked their own land, that is to say, peasants. It was not, in this respect, very different from the population of the same village in the middle of the nineteenth century, and probably not very dissimilar to that which witnessed the invasions of Caesar's legions. One is reminded of Fernand Braudel's conception of social evolution as slow, not to say immutable, consisting more of continuities than of ruptures.

But let us put aside these apparent permanencies. Several families stand out by their greater landed wealth or by their idle way of life. They did not till their own fields, but entrusted them to the labour of others, to other men. Herein lies our first difficulty: what was the status of these labourers? For generations of historians, they have been 'serfs' (from the Latin *servus*), that is a new juridical category, distinct from the slave and specific to a medieval society which was assumed to date back to the Germanic invasions, if not to the third century, that terrible century of Roman history. The more cautious, certainly, took refuge behind the expression 'non-free', or the formula *servi casati* (serfs settled on holdings). In sum, they were anything but slaves properly speaking, as if the ancient world had definitively ended and the persistence into the tenth century of a condition so inhumane was scarcely thinkable.

This view, it seems to me, must be revised. To prefer the word 'slave' to 'serf' as the translation of *servus* is not merely a quibble; we are faced with a fundamental question involving our global view of society. Was slavery still in the tenth century the most common way of utilising the labour of others, or not?

Slaves, not serfs

I will give first a few examples in order to convey the atmosphere of the sources. Antigius was a well-off landowner living in the hamlet of Varanges at the heart of the *ager* of Merzé.[1] In 935 he made a donation in favour of the monastery of Cluny: it consisted of various pieces of land (of which he retained the usufruct for life) and a family of *mancipia*, that is Vualmorus and his wife, their son Dominique and their daughter, whose name, like that of her mother, is not recorded. Not far away, in the same year and for the same stated reason (the salvation of their deceased parents), Arnaldus and his wife Aremburgis granted, on the same terms, a vineyard, a house (*mansio*) and a *servus* called Guntaldus, his wife and their children.[2] In a final example, Téza, a widow living at Collonge, made a gift in 940 of a piece of land, some *servi* and some *ancillae*.[3] The vocabulary of slavery is omnipresent in the cartulary: *servus* to designate the male, *ancilla* for the female, *mancipia* as a neuter collective. Those who drew up the acts could have adopted as their own the statement enunciated by one agent of Charlemagne: 'One is free or slave, nothing else'. For them, assuredly, things were quite clear.

A status of exclusion

And so they should be for us. The *servus* was first and foremost the property of his master, an element in his patrimony which he disposed of at will, in the same way as a field or some cattle. Between them was not a contract but a hereditary link, the servile bond (the *nexus servitutis* often quoted by the scribes). From this link derived the *servitium* due to the master, which meant that, in the words of Georges Duby, 'the master could demand anything of him, without owing him anything in return'.[4] Nowhere, in fact, do we see services or rents defined in any way, and the arbitrary power of the master seems to have been the rule. This probably differentiated such 'private' slaves from those attached to the royal or episcopal estates. Further, the slave was justiciable only to his master, even if the latter had lost the power of life and death, as a result of a long process which had begun in the Late Empire and been accentuated by Frankish legislation. 'Cattle with human faces', Marc Bloch's phrase, accurately sums up the weakness of the slave's juridical personality.

The second element of the slave condition was exclusion from the institutions of public law and the inability to participate in public life. The slave attended neither judicial assemblies, where his testimony was not admitted, nor the assemblies of men of arms. He could not enter the clergy in principle, and in practice no *servi* seem to appear amongst the numerous 'Levites' then present in rural society. Excluded from the state, he was similarly excluded from the village and hamlet communities; the 'common lands' of Lournand, Chevagny and Collonge, open to the exercise of common rights, were also called, significantly, 'terres des francs', that is the lands of the free men. This was probably the fundamental feature of the slave's juridical condition; servitude in the tenth century was above all a status of exclusion, as it had always been in classical antiquity. In this it clearly differed from the later 'serfdom'. The serf certainly suffered numerous juridical disabilities and his 'stain' (*macula*) was, like that of the slave, hereditary; but his acceptance within the rural community conferred on him a sort of 'minimal citizenship'; he may have been a 'nobody', but at least he was somebody.

The final element in the juridical character of the *servus* was his exclusion from property, as had always been the case in antiquity (the two exclusions – property and state – go together, as Moses Finley has shown).[5] This point merits particular attention, as it has been the subject of conflicting views. According to Georges Duby, the *servus* of the tenth century possessed 'allods', 'titles of ownership' and a 'distinct patrimony'.[6] Certain texts appear at first sight to support this. For example, a certain Eldinus, driven, we are told by famine, sold to the monks a curtilage and its dependencies within the territory of Merzé, for the sum of eighteen *sous* (a very large sum).[7] Eldinus was described as a *servus*, indeed the deed specified *servus sancti Petri*, with reference to the patron saint of the abbey; he was thus a *servus* of the abbey. Another example concerns Varanges in 935; when Antigius gave the abbey one of his 'curtilages', the confines were, as usual, enumerated.[8] We thus learn that to the west and north it adjoined the land of Daniel, *servus sancti Petri*, and on another side, the land of Otgarius, also a *servus sancti Petri*; Daniel and Otgarius must have been landowners, since in any other eventuality the scribe would have written 'the land of X or Y', then added '*ubi residet* [where lived] Daniel and Otgarius'.

Yet another *servus* of St Peter called Constancius, from the neighbouring locality of Massy, sold two pieces of vineyard to the monks, just as if he were free.[9] It will have been noted that each of these examples concerns not ordinary slaves belonging to private persons but slaves belonging to the abbey. However, when we turn to what was the most common condition, that of private slaves, their exclusion from ownership is obvious. Out of hundreds of land transactions, there is not one to which an ordinary *servus* is a party, nor one in which a slave of this type appears amongst the owners of adjoining land. When we look elsewhere in the Mâconnais we find the same. As a general rule, the slaves of the tenth century did not dispose of what can properly speaking be called a patrimony. Further, there is no trace of any contingent right of *mainmorte*, which they would have acquitted when transmitting their property, as did the later 'serfs'.

Changes in the servile condition

The situation in this regard remained wholly in line with antiquity, except that we see emerge with the slaves of the monastery (and probably also those of the king or count) a new servile condition which breaks with the traditional principle of exclusion. Men recently rescued from a personal dependence in favour of a less degrading link with a monastic community or prestigious institution – and, through them, with God – had acquired the right of ownership and thereby taken a step in the direction of a different status. This was a decisive development, clearly perceived as such by the compilers of the deeds. It is evident in the comment of one scribe when some young slaves (*servuli*) of Chevagny were given to the abbey in the early years of the tenth century: *ut servitutem nulli reddant homini, nisi soli Deo et Sancto Petro*,[10] and later, *ut ista liberatio vel donatio*. What was intolerable, the true crux of servitude, was enslavement to a man; entry into dependence on Cluny was perceived as an enfranchisement, since it conferred on the beneficiary a real juridical personality and essential rights.

Was this move towards a new condition of long standing? Nothing in the documentation for the Mâconnais makes it possible to tell. But one inevitably thinks of two famous documents concerning slavery, the Law of the Alamans and the Law of the Bavarians, both from the eighth century and probably inspired by legislation of Dagobert (seventh century).[11] They define the status of ecclesiastical slaves by reference to that of royal slaves, and fix the services and rents due from the plot of land assigned to them. Fixed obligations, however heavy, in place of an arbitrary *servitium*, represent a parallel evolution to that observed with regard to rights of ownership. So the change was probably old, but it concerned only a tiny minority of men whose birth had placed them in servitude, and it gradually created, in a complex dialectic between the old and the new, two distinct juridical conditions. It was probably in the vicinity of the old cities, on ecclesiastical or comital estates, where, that is, the immediate presence of the public authority could extenuate the weakening of the personal link, that the change began, and slaves who were no longer wholly slaves appeared. Unfortunately for the historian, almost all the sources available are of ecclesiastical origin, and the trap is set; what is perceived as the servile condition is in fact only an avatar. The advantage of our sample from the Mâconnais, remote from these exceptional conditions, becomes apparent: it reveals, I repeat, slaves, not serfs.

Was the slave a tenant?

I shall perhaps be reproached for an excessive legalism. What we see here is surely simply the juridical envelope, in a sense empty, of slavery, a deceptive gloss concealing new social realities. This is the argument of those who refuse to accept the persistence of slavery, with all its implications. It is the case, notably, with a particular Marxist tradition predicated on changes in the Late Empire, in the third century, and which sees as crucial (the change in the 'relations of production') the appearance of the Roman colonate and the settling on holdings of former slaves. The latter are thus already 'tenants', scarcely different from medieval serfs, and the real change lies in the substitution of small-scale, family-based production for the gang slavery practised on the great estates. This thesis is by no means negligible. In particular, it correctly stresses one key historical factor (though one neglected, not to say ignored, by contemporary historiography): the evolution of the nature of production. Feudalism was, in effect, the age par excellence of small-scale production, both rural and urban, the period when the narrow family group (the couple and their children) represented the basic unit of production, within which lay the essential division of labour. Failure to grasp this crucial fact makes it impossible to understand the very nature of the feudal system, since every one of its structures (from ideology to the social) was designed to buttress, protect and perpetuate small-scale production. By no means least in importance was the institution of the peasant holding, a mode of possessing land of exceptional stability, the indispensable cement in the link between the small producer and his means of production (the land). This apogee of small-scale production was, of course, the culmination of a very long process whose roots go far back in time, no doubt to the first agriculture, properly speaking, the history of which remains to be written (it would essentially be a history of family structures and productive forces). And we may note that feudalism, in pushing the process to its furthest point, inaugurated the reversal of the trend in the direction of an increasingly large-scale production, of increasingly 'social' character, as Marx would have put it.

It is clear that the history of slavery has to be re-located within this context. The installation of a servile family on a plot of land from which it drew its subsistence and which conferred on it the beginnings of autonomy was certainly an important stage. But let us not, for pity's sake, anticipate; one swallow does not make a summer; nor, in a capitalist society, does the nationalisation of a few major means of production or exchange create socialism. The social condition of the slave changed without slavery disappearing, just as workers' conditions have changed since the nineteenth century without it therefore being possible to assume the definitive disappearance of this class.

I repeat that to see the slave of the High Middle Ages as a tenant is to proceed too far too fast. Everyone knows that medieval peasant tenure follows from a sort of break with the property law inherited from Rome. To the one (the lord), the eminent rights, to the other (the peasant), the use rights or usufruct in return for rent, both parties seeing the land as theirs and transmitting their rights to their heirs. Was there anything of this sort in the Mâconnais before 1000? It is open to doubt. The one thing that is certain is the almost systematic installation of each servile family on a small or medium-sized exploitation: sometime a 'curtilage' and a few vines, sometimes a 'manse' or holding of larger size. Nothing justifies the assumption that the slave had any right over this land, nor, with even stronger reason, seeing it as a sort of *hereditas*. Close scrutiny of concrete situations leads rather to the opposite hypothesis. Let us suppose for the moment a hereditary transmission of use rights in these lands. We would inevitably observe, here and there, a second family unit installed on the same

land when one of the children (and they were numerous!) married
before the death of their parents. But, in twenty or so cases where the
evidence is excellent (detailed composition of the family group), not
one single one diverges from the rule: one complete family (father/
mother/children), and one only, on each holding. How are we to
explain the uniformity of this model, the homogeneity of circumstances, other than by regulation imposed by the master? Such regulation, indeed, must have been indispensable, since without it an absurd
economic situation would soon have been reached: too many people
on too small holdings, from which no further surplus could any longer
be squeezed. How could such regulation have been enforced other
than by the complete and simultaneous control over the devolution of
land on the one hand, and over the formation of new servile families
on the other?

The most likely solution to the difficult problem of the requisite
one-couple/one-holding equation is of childlike simplicity: it sufficed
to create new couples only as and when they were needed, that is when
holdings became vacant. The strict control exercised by the master
over the servile family receives additional confirmation from the total
absence of mixed (free/slave) marriages; in the *ager* of Merzé, every
servus was linked to an *ancilla*. To find the exception which proves the
rule, we have to turn to the slaves belonging to the count. In 996,
Alberic, count of Mâcon, gave to the abbey a female slave called Baya
with her children by a certain Giroldus, apparently a free man, since he
appears amongst the subscribers to the donation.[12] Once again we
observe the distinction between the ordinary fabric of rural society
and the situation unique to the public estates, lay or ecclesiastical. This
was probably a distinction of general application, when one thinks of
the impression of the 'great estate' given by the Carolingian polyptychs, where mixed marriages and the sub-division of manses were
common – which, furthermore, weakened this artificial construct.

Let us speak not of 'servile tenants' but rather of '*casati*' slaves, that
is, slaves settled on holdings. The tenth-century slave was not entrenched on a holding transmitted from generation to generation, as was
the later serf. No doubt it was in the interests of the master to keep him
on the same holding and sometimes even entrust it to one of the
children of a slave who died, so that over time the servile family would
come to see as its own the land on which they lived. The hereditary
tenure of the succeeding period would hardly be conceivable if such

practices had not previously been widespread. But, for the moment, the *servus* remained in the power of a master who disposed of him at will; he was a slave and nothing else.

The pillar of the social edifice

The expression 'slave society' can have two distinct meanings. In its looser sense, it is applied to any society practising slavery to a greater or lesser degree, in which case the use of the term hardly commits its author. This is not how it will be used here; we understand by it a society based on slavery as on a pillar, thus inconceivable without it. We will equally reject the view according to which the presence of slaves is only a remote survival, a social archaism, such as often occurs, without much significance. I would even have used the classical terminology of Marxism, by speaking of 'dominant relations of production', except that this formulation is singularly ambiguous. 'Dominant' on what plane? That of numbers? Of the volume of levies enjoyed by the ruling social elite? Of the volume of production assured by the servile labour force? Let us prudently confine ourselves to the study of social realities.

The problem of numbers

Let us begin with the problem of numbers, that is the percentage of slaves within rural society. It is an important, though a difficult, question. The problem at the documentary level is obvious: since land transactions involved only free men and landowners (including in the enumeration of the confines), they are over-represented in the sources. We will have occasion to return to this point later in respect of demography, but let us note at once that we are able to establish the names of something in the order of 90 per cent of the 'free men' living on these territories, either directly (in their capacity as donors or vendors) or indirectly (in their capacity as neighbours of the latter). The same is not true of slaves, who by definition do not figure in the documents except when they are the subject of gifts. So, one error leading to another, a failure to perceive that they are excluded from ownership leads automatically to an understatement of their number.

Arithmetical proof can easily be provided. Between 935 and 1022 (or the space of three generations), twenty-three servile families appear in the whole of the Lournand–Chevagny–Collonge–Cotte–

Merzé grouping (leaving aside the six families living at Varanges). Given that the global average population of this same grouping was between eighty-five and ninety families in the tenth century, we have, for all three generations, a stock of the order of 260 families; this suggests, at first sight, a servile population of the order of 8 per cent. But this is a pure optical illusion, since of the twenty-three servile families only five appear in the period 935–80 and eighteen in the period 980–1022. It is not that the servile population experienced a sudden growth; it is simply that donations of slaves to the abbey were rare up to the last quarter of the century, but the movement then accelerated, to peak around 1000. For a true picture, we need therefore to exclude the figures relating to the first period and retain the later ones, that is eighteen families for a span of a generation and a half, or twelve servile families per generation, that is very close to 15 per cent. This is, it should be emphasised, a minimum figure. Not all the servile families of this territory were given to the abbey, as is shown by several later donations. With 15 per cent, therefore, we have a minimum estimate for the year 1000, an estimate which should be corrected upwards for the first half of the tenth century in order to take account of the consequences, though limited, of the first donations. These are very rough estimates, to be sure, but they have the merit of conveying orders of magnitude and of avoiding the principal trap, that of underestimating.

Before drawing a conclusion from these figures, one last observation should be made on the spatial distribution of these twenty-three families; it could not be more uneven. The old Gallic village, the most populous of the group, had only two, and the neighbouring hamlets of Chevagny and Collonge three each, whereas the territory of Merzé alone had thirteen, and Cotte the last two. Slavery was to a degree concentrated in the valley of the Grosne at the junction of two successive colonisations, the Roman and the Germanic; we have, in fact, a microcosm, but two sectors or structures! We will have occasion to return more than once to this duality and its implications for economic and settlement history, since it is still visible in the contemporary landscape and agrarian structures.

The dominant form of dependent labour

That said, the slave class – even accepting a margin of error of 3 per cent – represented only a small minority. Did it cultivate between 20 and 25 per cent of the land? At the very most; most land was tilled not simply by free men, but by what we will now call peasant proprietors. In terms of production, slavery did not occupy a dominant position in the tenth century. However, it may well never have done so, even in Roman times. Nor should we, in terms of levies to the benefit of the dominant elite, overestimate the contribution of these small servile exploitations, which had to assure their own reproduction and probably produced only small surpluses. Can we therefore see them as an essential element in the social apparatus? Yes, as long as we appreciate their specific function. The possession of slaves was, for a small number of dominant families within the *ager* of Merzé, the instrument of a social hegemony which raised them above the rest of the free population and at the same time gave them access to other sources of revenue, either by the direct exploitation of these last or by the redistribution of church revenues. We will return to the configuration of this little local elite, bottom layer of the landed aristocracy and crucial articulation between the peasant communities and the surrounding society. Let us simply note for the moment that their landed wealth significantly exceeded that of the small and middling peasantry. The most modest of these 'large allod-holders' owned two or three exploitations, some as many as six or seven, some even more. None of them tilled their own fields or pruned their own vines. This was precluded by their conception of social life as much as by the dimensions of their landed patrimony. For them it was an imperative to have recourse to the labour of others.

What solutions were available? Of wage labour, we know almost nothing. If it existed, it can only have been on a small scale, at times of seasonal demand, and drawing on the services of men and women beset by poverty. There was nothing comparable to the modern wage-earner; nor was there a labour market. It is clear that free men were reluctant to work for others. Indirect proof is provided by the solution commonly adopted for the breaking up of uncultivated land: the contract of *complant*. The large allod-holder (for example, Arleius in 1002) called on the services of simple peasants (Winiterius, Gonbardus, Martinus and Constancius) who, at the end of the operation, retained as theirs half of the land assarted.[13] This was certainly, for them, a more honourable situation, but one employed only for exceptional projects.

There remained only dependent labour, performed by virtue of the constraint exercised by the master. Were men regarded as 'free' installed permanently on holdings? We find a few examples. Thus at Varanges, in 976, Magingodus gave to his wife a 'curtilage, a vineyard and a "demesne manse" where Valericus will live' (as the latter's juridical condition is not recorded, he was clearly 'free').[14]

More explicit is the act by which the heirs of Arleius granted two 'demesne manses' (we will return to the significance of this term) to the abbey in 981–2.[15] They included in the donation a couple of slaves and specified that the man called Evrardus (without reference to his juridical status) would hold one of the two manses for life. We thus learn that Arleius, a representative of one of the two principal local slave-owning families, on occasion entrusted one of his holdings to a free man and further that the commitment made to him was for life, with a sufficiently strong customary value for it not to be cancelled by the transfer of the property. Evrardus thus became a 'free' dependant of the abbey. We are at this point very close to medieval tenure. Only hereditary transmission by right is lacking; perhaps the fact already preceded the law.

That said, recourse to installing 'free tenants' (or *coloni*, to use the classic generic term) remained exceptional: one case out of ten, at most, on the lands of the small local aristocracy. This was a further contrast with the situation attributed to the large Carolingian estate, on which *coloni* were more numerous than *servi*. This should come as no surprise; the installation and retention of such *coloni* in an appreciable number supposed the presence of a strong public authority – such as that exercised by a count or bishop – to which Arleius could not pretend. The link binding Evrardus to him was clearly private; it derived from the old *commendatio* of Merovingian origin. Evrardus, or one of his ancestors, at the end of his tether, had one day made himself dependent on and placed himself under the protection of a more powerful person, and received, in return, a holding to cultivate. In law he remained 'free', but in practice his condition was close to the servile condition. The error, however, is to see this as a frequent solution and imagine ancient servitude progressively submerged under the rising tide of a new dependence.

For the large local landowners the normal method of cultivating the land is perfectly clear: the slave or, more precisely, the servile couple sufficed. To be somebody, to be a person of distinction within that society, required possession of one or several such couples. This was the only way to avoid having to wield a spade or drive a plough, for which activities it was impossible not to feel a certain repugnance by reason of the already thousand-year-old charge of the servile ideology. It was also the only way to escape the narrow horizons of village or hamlet life and enter public life in its military, judicial or religious aspects. The majority of free men, in fact, aspired to this condition. If they did not possess slaves, it was simply because they could not. However, the attraction of the model was so strong that one finds small or middling landowners with landed possessions of only modest size keeping a servile family to hand in order to ensure their cultivation. Such situations were marginal, aberrant from the economic standpoint, but significant, nevertheless, on the mental plane.

In this sense, slavery remained the dominant relation of exploitation, even if the slave made only a small contribution to global production. Slavery was dominant to the extent that other forms of exploiting the labour of others, still in gestation, were confined to a subsidiary role. An ideological transformation, radically modifying views of labour and doing away with the antagonistic liberty/servitude coupling, would be necessary to prepare the ground for a new form of exploitation, in the event, for the 'feudal rent' (or seigneurial levy) demanded of tenants. To suggest, with Chris Wickham, that the revenues of the aristocracy of the High Middle Ages reposed principally on feudal rent make sense only if the great estates alone are taken into account.[16] There, in effect, free tenants or *coloni* were numerous, and the slaves themselves appear as tenants burdened with rents and thus placed in a relation assimilable to a pre-seigneurial relation. The assertion is equally valid for the upper ranks of the aristocracy, that is for an extremely narrow social group. To extend it to the lesser aristocracy rooted in the land is, in the case of the Mâconnais, totally unjustifiable. The dominant class was surely not the small group of great lords taken in isolation but an aristocracy forming a coherent whole, which had the small local masters as an indispensable bottom layer. This was a stratum which was based on servile labour (in the absence of any other solution), which was, in consequence, the veritable pillar of the social edifice.

The decline of slavery?

Did this pillar stand firm or did it, on the contrary, reveal signs of weakness? The question assumes a particular importance if the conclusions above are accepted. Indeed, it becomes a key question to the understanding of the social dynamic. Should the rise, and soon the generalisation, of new forms of exploitation (seigneurial or 'feudal') be attributed to an eventual decline of slavery? Or, if preferred, is the master/slave contradiction at the heart of the historical process which modified Frankish society and paved the way for feudal society? Such a complex problem must be approached with the utmost caution. We are not presented with a simple master/slave confrontation; alongside them, an independent peasantry continued to play a role. There is no justification for isolating the servile relationship and its evolution from the wider context within which it existed.

From Marc Bloch to Pierre Bonnassie

We should, nevertheless, begin by considering, from an analytical perspective, the dynamic of the servile relationship. Was it in decline, and if so, which factors were exerting influence? These questions, as Pierre Bonnassie observed in a recent article, have been a perpetual embarrassment to historians.[17] In the great syntheses of social history, they are usually neglected, if not ignored. Rare have been the authors conscious of the importance of this problem. Overall, since the 1930s, there have been only three amongst French historians, that is one per generation.

It was Marc Bloch who, in a famous article,[18] opened the debate. He diagnosed a gradual decline of slavery between the fifth and the ninth centuries and the emergence of a new condition, serfdom, encompassing old slaves and impoverished free persons alike. He primarily discussed the causes of this process, emphasising the minor role played by the Church, the subsidiary role of military and political factors, and the importance of the economic factor: the masters thought in terms of economic profitability, first preferring the solution of settling slaves on holdings to that of direct maintenance, then inclining towards enfranchisement, which transformed the slave into a free or half-free tenant. This produced a sort of slow evaporation of slavery which gradually modified the face of rural society.

The next phase was dominated by the work of Georges Duby. From the spate of ideas so characteristic of it, I will note here only what perhaps constitutes his decisive contribution, which substantially revised our view of medieval society: the concept of a feudal revolution around the year 1000.[19] For the first time, the decisive importance of this rupture was brought out, even if, from the pen of this historian, the illumination remained primarily political and ideological, and even if he displayed some hesitation and unease with regard to the relationship between slavery and serfdom. But a door had been unbolted.

The third major contribution, more recent, is that of Pierre Bonnassie, in the direct tradition of Marc Bloch and Georges Duby. His article caused great excitement in the academic world. No, he said, in essence, slavery persisted throughout the High Middle Ages, even if it was in retreat, a retreat to which he applied, with refinements, the problematic of Marc Bloch. Thanks to Pierre Bonnassie, the dossier has been reopened and new life breathed into the debate. Here and there, scholars are once again addressing the issue and looking more closely at their sources. In the case of the Mâconnais, the persistence of slavery is patent, and I am in full agreement with Pierre Bonnassie. There remains the question of slavery's retreat or decline.

The decline of slavery or the upgrading of slaves?

What is meant by the 'decline' of slavery? Should its evolution from the fifth to the tenth centuries be posed in these somewhat ambiguous terms? If it is simply a question of identifying a reduction in the number of slaves, and a consequent diminution of their global role in society, nothing is less obvious, all remains to be proved.

Let us return to the figure proposed above, that is a minimum of 15 per cent slaves in the tenth century, a percentage which at first sight appears small. Are there grounds for seeing this as a sort of residue surviving at the end of a long erosion of the servile stock? We have no reference point for the preceding centuries, so we cannot offer a precise answer based on figures. But we can argue on the basis of what is known about social structure. We know – a point to which we will return – that there existed in the tenth century, alongside the slave-owning sector, a small landowning peasantry which accounted for over half of the cultivated area. These peasant communities had survived the High Middle Ages, with its civil wars, famines and aggression by the powerful. To attribute to them in the previous centuries a position at least equal to that observed for the tenth is not so much wildly daring as simple good sense. It follows that a percentage of slaves significantly higher than 15 is quite inconceivable since it would be incompatible with the social structure. At most, and not out of any desire for paradox, if a hypothesis as to the evolution of the number of slaves has to be hazarded, there are more reasons to posit an increase – parallel with the progress of the large estate – than a reduction.

On what can the thesis of the 'decline' of slavery be based? On references to enfranchisement or the possible difficulties of recruitment? These are far from convincing arguments, since renewal of the servile labour force (a crucial aspect of the 'social reproduction' of the system) was quite simply effected by the natural movement of births. The servile family, contrary to received wisdom, was relatively fertile. So as to avoid arguing on the basis of too restricted a sample of families, let us use the data assembled by André Deléage for a wider area.[20] He deducted thirty-four unmarried persons from 135 households (that is, one unmarried person per four households). Of the 135 households, we know in eighty-seven cases the number of children (in the other cases, the scribe put simply 'and their children'). The figures are as follows: only seven without children, twenty with one, twenty-two with two, sixteen with three, eight with four, nine with five, three with six, two with more than six. This represents nearly three living children (2.9 to be precise) per household with children, which represents a birth rate amply sufficient to ensure the reproduction of the servile population and even permit, in addition, some enfranchisements. These figures, we should note in passing, ought to make us ponder the existence of a 'servile' demographic system, inasmuch as exclusion from landownership meant that these populations did not suffer constraints analagous to those affecting the free. At all events, to speak of a drying up of the supply of slaves makes no sense here. When describing the near-disappearance of slavery in the eleventh century, it has sometimes been assumed that it resulted from a growing scarcity of the sources of supply. But slavery did not disappear because of a shortage of slaves; the settling of slaves on holdings, by giving a material base to the conjugal unit, was in itself enough to make possible the maintenance, perhaps even the growth, of the servile stock.

Let us therefore avoid the ambiguity of the word 'decline' to express the dynamic affecting slavery. It is in qualitative rather than quantitative terms that the question should be posed, in terms of the amelioration of the servile condition or the upgrading of slaves, with for vector the original contradiction of this condition: the slave was a human being, on whom a status of 'sub-humanity' had been imposed, to employ the formula of Pierre Bonnassie,[21] 'a tool with a voice' as Aristotle had earlier expressed it. The conflict between these two dimensions, opposed and inseparable, dominates the history of this social category. In certain historical conditions, when enslavement proceeded essentially from conquest, the status of sub-humanity could be imposed in all its rigour, and found its ultimate expression in the 'gang slavery' of the estates of colonial type created over a wide area by Rome. But the other dimension, the human face, never ceased to emerge, from the period of the Late Empire, in the class wars which took a wide variety of forms, violent or non-violent. The new historical conditions which resulted from the 'barbarian' invasions accelerated this trend. Henceforward, various factors, cumulatively effective, favoured the upgrading of slaves, factors which there is little point in attempting to rank, so closely are they interconnected.

Nor should we neglect the religious factor. The argument, so frequently repeated, that the Church played no role in this process is surely a gross oversimplification. Certainly, the Church remained, as a body, slave-owning to the last. The famous poem by Adalbero of Laon in the form of an admonition to Robert the Pious was simply, in practice, a last defence of the social status quo and the retention of *servi* (slaves, not serfs!) in their condition, at the very moment when things were disintegrating before its author's eyes.[22] The teaching of the Church never ceased to repeat the arguments of Sts Paul and Augustine: let each remain in his condition, slavery being the punishment for sin. And the practice was not confined to the ideological plane; slaves were too necessary to the cultivation of the ecclesiastical estates.

But we should surely not leave it at that and ignore the effects of the gradual penetration of Christianity into the depths of rural society. It responded to an ideological necessity, if only with regard to the servile world. But whether intended or not, it set in motion uncontrollable consequences by its gradual creation of a religious community which transcended juridical frontiers. One would like to know when slaves first crossed the threshold of the church at

Lournand or the chapel at Collonge.* It is difficult to draw any conclusion from the very restricted dimensions of this tiny chapel. In the case of the church in the hamlet of Merzé, a majority of whose population was servile, the foundations have never been excavated. In the tenth century, at any rate, these slaves were indubitably Christian and we should note that the disappearance of slavery at the end of the century was inseparable from the activities of Cluny, underpinned by a more demanding spirituality,

The slave, what is more, had a family, a Christian family. 'His marriage was a Christian marriage', as Georges Duby observed, and his children were baptised,[23] which made for a stable structure; this was a crucial factor whose implications we perhaps fail to appreciate; the dignity of the slave family drew strength from it. Kinship and family structures remain an obscure chapter in our history, which the too exclusively structural readings of today do not always help to illumine. The family, as a historic category, cannot be studied apart from its social levels. The servile family was well and truly specific, even if its aspect as a narrow conjugal family gave it a close resemblance to the dominant model provided by the society of the 'free'. Its specificity derived from the control exercised over it by the master with clearly defined ends in view: to produce, certainly, but also to reproduce, in the strict sense of the term. Celibacy was limited by the absence of other social perspectives, the age of marriage probably determined by the economic needs of the master, fertility unbridled by the absence of constraints of a patrimonial order. We are here at the heart of the sub-humanity/humanity contradiction. The practice of a sort of servile stock farming corresponded to the former, but, in requiring a stable conjugal unit, it promoted the latter and ameliorated the servile condition. The effects of acculturation produced by the proximity of the free and the practice of a common faith no dount completed the process of the assimiliation of the two respective family models. We should take care, therefore, to avoid the temptation of a facile anti-clericalism. Christianity was no doubt, in spite of itself (in spite of its 'doctors'), a powerful factor in the upgrading of slaves.

---

* This tiny, pre-Romanesque chapel still survives, apparently without having experienced any significant alterations; it measures 10.15 by 6.7 metres externally, with an internal area of some 40 square metres.

This in no way, of course, detracts from the role of economic and social factors. The decisive event in this regard was the settling on holdings of servile families. This conferred on its beneficiaries the beginnings of economic autonomy and intensified, by the same token, the sub-humanity/humanity contradiction. These 'beginnings' – the word needs to be emphasised, since the road was long (not only for slaves but also for small free peasant producers) – led on to the peasant of the feudal system, a thousand times more autonomous by reason of the stability he had acquired as regards his possession of land, the numerous institutional and mental agencies which protected small production and, lastly – a point to which we will return – by reason of a phenomenon destined to transform the life of the peasant and increase his autonomy, the opening up of the rural market. But the route had been mapped out, the progress was irreversible; settling slaves on holdings produced cumulative effects, giving them weapons, and engendering new rights. The crucial context from which slaves were able, in the very long term, to benefit was thus the gradual affirmation of small-scale production based on the family unit as the most efficient form of production. Behind this can be detected, in the last analysis, the progress of the 'productive forces', to the extent that it permitted restricted human units to break free from wider economic solidarities.

The connection between technical progress and the end of slavery thus seems to be real, not as a factor producing immediate mechanical consequences but as a background condition operating through a number of different mediations.[24] We should not, however, cling to the idea that the technological innovations of the High Middle Ages precipitated a decline of slavery by valorising free labour, whilst forced labour was revealed as increasingly inefficient and unsuitable to respond to technological progress. This idea proceeds from a moral judgement, well meaning no doubt, but with little contact with reality. In the first place, the logic is not one of decline but rather one of social promotion. Secondly, we have no reason to think or claim that the slave was less productive than the free person. This, surely, is a received idea. There will be opportunity, when discussing technical progress, to develop the opposite view; slaves were associated with the most dynamic sector of the economy. Further, they had since antiquity been the bearers of a technical tradition certainly superior to that of free men, thanks to the latter's prejudices against 'mechanical' labour and activities. It is highly likely that slaves worked as much as, and as well, if not better than, the surrounding peasantry, impelled as they were by the feeling that the gulf between them and the others was tending to diminish. It would perhaps not be anachronistic to compare their behaviour to that of so many immigrants in the developed societies of today, gradually reducing, at the price of a sometimes manic labour, the distance separating them from the lower levels of the host society.

This conception also explains, let us note, the absence of open conflicts between masters and slaves. We find, in effect, nothing similar to the great slave revolts of the third and fourth centuries (the Bacaudae) in what was, the evidence suggests, a very different context. There is even no sign of the slave escapes described by Pierre Bonnassie for Catalonia,[25] though it may well be that our sources alone explain this silence. If, however, such problems occurred, it has to be said that they altogether failed to disrupt the economy of the masters. The class struggle took other forms; it was neither spectacular nor violent, as some have liked to imagine. It was above all a long march towards social dignity and status; and it was victorious.

On the threshold of integration

This is the first element in our analysis: it was a society still based on slavery, in continuity therefore (despite the importance of the changes experienced since the invasions of the fifth century) with ancient society. But it was also a society whose dominant relation of exploitation had become fragile; all major social systems are sooner or later faced with this central problem. This had been the case, indeed, with ancient society in the third century, with the crisis of traditional slavery. It had found a durable solution in the settling of slaves on holdings, in, that is, a profound reordering of the 'relation of production'; the obvious drawback, fatal in the long term, was that it emphasised the 'humanity' of the slave. We are here at the end of the process; on the eve of the year 1000, the slave had reached the threshold of integration. We should not be surprised at the length of these historical processes; it is inherent in the complexity, the multiple coherences, and thus the almost inexhaustible resistence, of a social system whose prime historical virtue was its force of inertia. Without making too many concessions to the historical fashions of today, let us note the obvious: slavery was not only a 'relation of production', but also a mentality which impregnated all social classes and groups, slaves included. It was already a thousand years old, and it is difficult to see what other mentality could have replaced it, and at what point, before the year 1000.

That said, the threshold in question had not yet been crossed. We will not at this point examine this privileged moment, for the simple reason that the slaves did not cross it alone. Important though their role in this development was (even if their participation was silent), it was inseparable from what was taking place at other levels of the social edifice. That, surely, is characteristic of all revolutions.

Lastly, the problem of slavery is like many other historical problems in that their solution long eludes us because the problem is not, to begin with, posed in the correct terms. We have thus persisted in considering slavery in isolation, pondering the causes of its disappearance on the a priori assumption that one element of the structure could have disappeared independently of the rest. This was a false start, which has succeeded in confusing the issue and led to the ante-dating of the disappearance of slavery. It was perhaps also the result of a conceptual weakness linked to the refusal to identify a social whole. The real issue, in my view, is not that of the end of slavery but that of the end of a slave system taken in its entirety. After the year 1000, the element was swept away along with everything else.

Notes

1 C. C. 428.
2 C. C. 431.
3 C. C. 517.
4 Duby, La Societé . . . dans la région mâconnaise, p. 113.
5 Moses Finley, The Ancient Economy, London, 1973, pp. 62–3.
6 Duby, La Société . . . dans la région mâconnaise, p. 114.
7 C. C. 2431.
8 C. C. 429.
9 C. C. 954.
10 C. C. 2220.
11 Monumenta Germaniae Historica, Legum Sectio, vol. 5, Hanover, 1888 and 1926.
12 C. C. 1199.
13 C. C. 2256.
14 C. C. 1425.
15 C. C. 1580.
16 Chris Wickham, 'The other transition: from the Ancient World to Feudalism', Past and Present, CIII, 1984, pp. 3–36; Wickham places the rupture brought about by the primacy of feudal rent between the fourth and sixth centuries.

17 Bonnassie, 'Survival and extinction'.
18 Marc Bloch, 'Comment et pourquoi finit l'esclavage antique', *Annales-ESC*, 1947, reprinted in his *Mélanges historiques*, vol. I, Paris, 1963, and in *Slavery and Serfdom in the Middle Ages*, translated by W. R. Beer, Berkeley, 1975, pp. 1–31.
19 Duby, *La Société . . . dans la région mâconnaise*.
20 Deléage, *Vie rurale en Bourgogne*.
21 Bonnassie, 'Survival and extinction'.
22 C. Carozzi, 'Le "Carmen ad Rotbertum regem" d'Adalbéron de Laon', unpublished thesis, University of Paris IV, 1973.
23 Duby, *La Société . . . dans la région mâconnaise*, p. 124..
24 There is a useful critique of the 'economist' approach in Pierre Dockès, *La Libération médiévale*, Paris, 1979, pp. 145–85 (translated by Arthur Goldhammer as *Medieval Slavery and Liberation*, Chicago, 1982).
25 Pierre Bonnassie, *La Catalogne du milieu du Xe à la fin du XIe siècle: croissance et mutation d'une société*, Toulouse, 1975.

2
Social structure: the persistence of ancient principles

The vast majority of the rural population consisted of people considered to be free. They were, however, far from equal. A wide spectrum of actual conditions emerges from our sources. It ranges from the smallest (not to say wretched) *colonus* who cultivated the land of another to a tiny group of the well-off – who could be counted on the fingers of one or two hands – who formed the first layer of the aristocracy, or the point of local insertion of the dominant social stratum; in between lay a middling class of peasant-landowners, itself very differentiated. It was, in brief, an extremely hierarchical society, and was no doubt criss-crossed by numerous networks of dependence and dominance, on which one would like to throw, or be able to throw, light, with a view to understanding the mechanisms by which the hierarchies were 'reproduced', that key problem of social history.

Does it make sense to lump together such a heterogeneous group? The free had in common only their juridical condition, for many in practice a fiction. The historian perhaps risks falling into the same trap as that set by the dominant ideology, with aggravating circumstances for the Marxist historian, anxious to give due weight to the class realities underlying the status categories. But ideological though it may have been, the notion of freedom, or rather the antagonistic coupling liberty/servitude, expressed, while it deformed, a social reality, and it had an essential function which was indispensable to the coherence of the social whole. The wretched *colonus* whose unenviable lot we referred to above had every day before his eyes the spectacle of a neighbouring slave whose status was ignominious, not to say non-existent. He derived from this a certain pride, a feeling, or an illusion, of holding a certain rank inasmuch as he was free, as do poor whites in the developed societies of today in the presence of black immigrants. Let us be in no doubt: this image gave him comfort and helped him bear his lot. Far from being obsolete, this major social frontier retained its power and function in the tenth century. This must be our starting point.

This point alone, it should be said at the outset, is sufficient to discredit the use of the notion of feudal society, even prudently equipped with the prefix 'pre-', except in defiance of the most elementary rules of scholarly rigour. Feudal society was constructed in the eleventh century, throughout the whole of Europe, on new bases; its classes were not the same; its social imagery, that is, the famous tripartite division into *oratores* (those who prayed), *milites* (those who fought) and *laboratores* (those who worked), had nothing in common with what preceded it; its social frontiers were differently located, thereby indicating that the changes were not a matter of form but resulted from a vast recomposition of the social. Of course, the new society did not spring suddenly from nowhere; an interminable period of gestation preceded its birth. Many elements were gradually put into place before coming together to form a new social system. But a rupture there clearly was. It would be unnecessary to insist on this were it not for the fact that, the work of several historians, including Georges Duby, notwithstanding, the majority of 'medievalists' fly in the face of the evidence, and prefer to preserve the myth of a Middle Ages extending from the fall of the Roman Empire to the discovery of America. To recognise the rupture of the tenth century strikes a heavy blow to numerous works, even recent, and, what is more, reduces the traditional territory of the medievalist by at least half – an argument which brooks no contradiction!

And if society was not as yet feudal, was this not perhaps a society functioning on the principles of ancient society (or societies)?[1] The existence, above the servile world, of a status group composed of 'citizen-landowners' is surely precisely one of the principle characteristics of such societies. It is, as yet, too soon to answer the question, but at the beginning of this chapter it needs to be posed.

A community of status: citizens and landowners

The vast majority of the 'free' of the 'High Middle Ages', after the fashion of their Roman and Greek predecessors, were, indeed, citizens and landowners, the two inseparable. The word 'citizen' may offend; it is not, of course, used in the formal definition inherited from Rome but in its wider meaning. The free man participated by right and by duty in public life. He was recognised by the public institutions common to the Carolingian world and still in place though in an advanced state of decay.[2] He participated to varying degrees in their operation, in the first place in the local judicial assembly which met in the chief settlement of the *ager*, the basic circumscription within the *pagus* or county. The way in which each deed specifies the location of the property being transmitted (in such and such a *pagus*, in such and such an *ager*, in such and such a *villa*, in the place called X) shows how these administrative and judicial structures persisted in men's minds, even if their effectiveness – as we will see when we examine the structural framework – was far from obvious. Their eclipse in favour of the parish as the new form of spatial perception did not become effective until the first third of the eleventh century. We need hardly emphasise here this further contrast with the future feudal society; the participation of the 'free' in public life, as structuring principle of society, would be reduced almost to extinction when the principal element in the population (the dependent peasantry), losing its judicial and military rights, was relegated to a sort of 'limited citizenship', exercised within the context of rural communities based essentially on agrarian solidarities of a technical order. This was a change indeed.

They were also landowners. By right, all of them; in reality, almost all. They bought, sold and exchanged land. They transmitted it to their heirs (according to a rule of strict equality), constituted dowries and dowers and, if the need arose, mortgaged their lands to contract a debt. In a word, they were, according to medieval terminology, 'allod-holders' or possessors of 'allods'. The word, of Germanic origin, has here lost its original meaning of family property to merge with the Roman concept of *proprietas*. The allod was thus land over which its owner enjoyed almost complete juridical power, unlike the 'tenure' to be discussed below. The compilers of the deeds used various but equivalent formulas to indicate this type of possession of land: sometimes even the word allod (*in alodo*), sometimes heritage (*hereditas*), or the expression *res juris nostri*. For the most part, they were content to define the concrete nature of the property without specifying its juridical status, regarding the latter as obvious. Thus they referred to the sale or gift of, for example, a field, a meadow or a vineyard. In the same spirit, they spoke of a 'manse', a *'colonge'* (*colonia*) or a 'curtilage'. The last thing we should see here, by analogy with the manse of the polyptychs, is different types of tenure: each of these terms, whose content was strictly economic, indicated in a broad sense a rural exploitation (that is, a group of parcels) and, more often, in a narrow sense the headquarters of this exploitation, that is the residence, any dependencies and the garden.

It is difficult to establish with any confidence what nuances are implied by the choice of words. The manse seems to have been more important than the curtilage; the word, derived from the Latin *manere* (to reside), emphasises in particular the presence of a house. It is in this sense that we understand the donation made to the abbey by a modest allod-holder of a curtilage with a 'demesne manse' (*cum manso indominicato*) and a little meadow and field adjoining;[3] this was probably a house of a certain quality, worthy of a master. The word '*colonge*' certainly refers to the original allocation of the Roman period, and it is hardly surprising to find it used frequently within the territory of Collonge, in close proximity to a Gallo-Roman villa. This word, too, has no implication for tenure. We see, for example, a certain Ingelardus give to the church of Merzé a *colonia* in which he retained a life interest: this was an allod transformed into a tenure on the occasion of a donation.[4]

This is our first finding: the majority of the rural population consisted of landowners who could dispose of and alienate their property at will. This should come as no surprise, since one of the principal achievements of medieval historiography over the last twenty years has been to demonstrate the importance of the allod as a mode of possession of land and emphasise the role of the small peasantry, hitherto so neglected. It is therefore on the allod that we should now focus our attention. Frankish society was based on it, as feudal society would later be based on the tenure, in other words on a mode of appropriation of the land which separated, for the same property, the eminent ownership from enjoyment of use rights.

The problems posed by the allod are many. We need to know how they were distributed, within the juridical group of free men, between small and large allod-holders; this is a question which will be tackled later, with our examination of the social hierarchies. Beforehand, two other points should be clarified: firstly, the place of the allod properly speaking within our territory, or, if preferred, the place of private property compared with the property of the Church or state (the count); and secondly, the modes of circulation of the allod. By what route were allods acquired – by inheritance, gift or purchase? Was there a process of concentration or accumulation of land in certain hands? Our opinion as to the cohesion or fragility of the social system will clearly depend on the answers to these questions.

The role of the allod

All historians of the Mâconnais, from Charmasse to Gracianskij, from André Deléage to Georges Duby, have addressed the question of the role of the allod. We will start with the two principal conclusions which have been reached. André Deléage proposed for the Cluny region in the mid tenth century the following estimate: one third, lands of the Church, between half and two thirds, private land.[5] Georges Duby, on the other hand, emphasised in particular the trend or evolution, observing a 'dissolution of allod wealth'.[6] Does our micro-analysis confirm these conclusions?

It can only provide, it must be admitted at the outset, rough and debatable estimates. The only possibility of a quantitative approach lies in making use of the fact that for every land transaction, through the enumeration of the confines, we know the rank of the neigh-bouring owners (except when the boundary of a parcel takes the form of a watercourse, slope, road or wall). It is, therefore, tempting to base on them statistics which should give a fairly accurate picture of the distribution of land.[7] Table 1 records the results. In order to refine the analysis, the figures have been distributed between four separate groups: on the one hand, the three principal communities (Lournand, Chevagny and Collonge), on the other, the group of small territorial units in the valley of the Grosne (Merzé, Cotte and Mailly). The lands of the Church have been sub-divided into four categories: those belonging to the abbey of Cluny, the cathedral of Mâcon, the local parish churches and lastly, under the heading of 'miscellaneous', the property of other more or less distant religious houses (Saint-Marcel of Chalon, Saint-Etienne of Lyons etc.). Lastly, the material has been grouped into two chronological periods, 910–75 and 976–1035, so as to reveal any possible trend.

At first sight, the overall total appears to show a higher proportion of ecclesiastical land (45 per cent) than that suggested by André Deléage. But this contradiction is more apparent than real. By definition, the cartulary of Cluny contains almost exclusively deeds concerning transactions made by the monks. They were constantly on the look-out for opportunities to concentrate or regroup their posses-sions. The parcels they coveted generally adjoined their own property

Table 1 Private and Church land, 910–75 and 976–1035 (%)

	Lournand	Chevagny	Collonge	Cotte, Merzé, Mailly	Total
910–95					
private land	33	26	47	37	143 (55.4)
land of the abbey of Cluny	31 (42.4)	22 (41.5)	16 (22.5)	17 (27.8)	86 (33.3)
land of the cathedral church	1	2	1	2	6 (2)
land of local churches	3	2	0	0	5 (1.9)
miscellaneous	5	1	7	5	18 (6.97)
total of Church lands	40	27	24	24	115 (44.5)
general total	73	53	71	61	258 (100)
976–1035					
private land	23	38	17	73	151 (53.9)
lands of the abbey of Cluny	21 (43.7)	12 (21.8)	30 (58.8)	42 (33.37)	105 (37.5)
lands of the cathedral church	0	0	0	4	4 (1.4)
lands of local churches	3	1	0	4	8 (2.8)
miscellaneous	1	4	4	3	12 (4.2)
total of Church lands	25	17	34	53	129 (46)
general total	48	55	51	126	280 (100)
910–1035					
private lands (%)	46.3	59.2	52.5	58.8	55
Church lands (%)	53.7	40.7	47.5	41.1	45

or were even sometimes surrounded by it, so that, when the confines were listed, the number of lands belonging to 'St Peter' (patron of the abbey) was artificially inflated, to a significant degree. It is true that, in contrast, the patrimony of Saint-Vincent of Mâcon is perhaps underestimated. However, the preponderance of Church land belonging to Cluny (about four-fifths) was such that the distortion has repercussions for the whole. There would be little point in claiming to introduce a reliable corrective to the treatment of these figures. Let us say only that the estimate of Deléage (33 per cent) is probably fairly close to the truth. It already reveals the scale of the territorial upheaval experienced since the beginning of the century and the arrival of the monks. We will have occasion later to look more closely at the stages and itinerary of their territorial ventures, but we can already observe a first phase dominated by penetration into Lournand and Chevagny, whereas after 975 Cotte and Merzé became their favoured targets. This needs to be explained.

Table 1 reveals a further increase in the landed wealth of the Church between the first and second periods, but it was apparently slight (from 44 to 46 per cent). The rate of increase was, in practice, more rapid, since our figures are subject to a further distortion. The penetration of the monks into Cotte and Merzé was of a different character from that into the other territorial units; in a more socially resistent milieu, it did not result in the formation of compact blocks of land, as in Lournand and Chevagny, but in the acquisition of more scattered properties surrounded by those of lay owners, which produced a small proportion of confines belonging to St Peter and a mitigation of the exaggerating effect referred to above.

Let us note simply the order of magnitude: the lands of the Church (essentially, that is, those of Cluny) represented a good third of the cultivated land towards the middle of the tenth century, and significantly more (40 per cent?) after the year 1000. Belonging to the Church, they were inalienable except by confiscation or usurpation. This whole sector escaped the grasp of private ownership and was exploited in ways we will examine later.

Other parts of the village territories also escaped this mode of appropriation: the 'common' lands or lands of the '*francs*'. We will not get involved here in the great debate about their origins, since our documentation brings no new information. They were probably very ancient, since we see collective control persist to our own day despite the upheavals consequent upon the establishment of seigneurial structures. Thus a part of the wood of Cotte was common; it remains common today, subject to the practice of firebote. More striking is the example of the meadows on the banks of the Grosne described as 'terres des francs of Chevagny'; in 1989 not only were they communally owned but the profits from their use were reserved for expenditure specific to the hamlet of Chevagny. The identity of the ancient hamlet communities has thus been maintained in customary fashion within contemporary administrative frameworks (the organisation of firebote, another illustration, is still based on this principle, each hamlet cutting its own woods).

It is impossible to determine the extent of these common lands.[8] Let us note only that they existed in each territorial unit and that they consisted of two principal elements: firstly, a part of the woodland, the rest being in the hands of the large allod-holders; secondly, water meadows on either side of the Grosne. They were reserved for the use of the free (to the exclusion of slaves), for whom they represented an indispensable complement to their private land. There they found the wood and timber necessary for heating, for the building and repair of their houses, and for the manufacture of their tools, and also a wide range of other resources (game, wild fruit, honey etc.). They also found supplementary food for their animals, especially pigs. The commons thus constituted a reservoir of resources, without which the economic equilibrium of these communities would soon have been broken.

The land owned by the small or larger landowners accounted for the rest, or almost, of the territory. Almost, since we have to discount a few properties held of the count of Mâcon. Thus, around the year 1000, we see a modest allod-holder of Lournand, Isenbrannus, grant all his property to the abbey, with the exception of the manse burdened with the *servitium* due to the count. The scribe first wrote *censum*, then struck it out and substituted *servitium*.[9] The word *beneficium* (benefice) was not used, but it was probably a small tenure of this type burdened with an honourable service. The other example is later (1030) and concerns Chevagny: the count granted to the abbey property from his inheritance which was held by Stephen (and before him by his father, Artaldus) *in beneficio* (as a benefice).[10] This was apparently noble tenure; we are here present at the birth of the hereditarily transmitted fief. But there are no grounds for projecting this situation back into the preceding century. Like the bishop and chapter, the count was not an important landowner here on the edge of his county, too far from Mâcon to be truly worthy of attention in his eyes. This remark applies equally to the four or five great aristocratic lineages of the Mâconnais, who are barely represented in the vicinity of Cluny.

This then, roughly speaking, was the allodial sector. If we exclude the wooded margins and various wastes, and take into account only the cultivated area, it amounted to nearly two-thirds of the area under consideration. Certainly, it was threatened by Cluniac penetration, and shrinking steadily, but in the mid tenth century it was still dominant. The allod accordingly represented one of the major bases of the social system. We have, it is true, for the moment included in the allodial sector very different social realities (small allod-holders and large slave-owning allod-holders), which we must soon distinguish and separate.

The solidity of the allodial sector

But, before doing so, we need to extend our analysis of this mode of land ownership in order to estimate its solidity. How did land pass from hand to hand? Did there exist a land market capable of exercising a bipolarising effect (accumulation of property at one pole, poverty at the other) to the benefit of those with more luck or greater ability? To find out, let us start with the findings of Georges Duby, whose conclusion is clear:

The circulation of money and merchandise seems not to have modified significantly the position of individuals or even of families within the economic hierarchy . . . on the other hand, pious donations and division by inheritance profoundly altered the distribution of wealth . . . alms were one of the most natural acts in this Christian society, inspired not so much by a particularly elevated sentiment of charity, as by the desire to purchase salvation.[11]

Let us express the same idea more generally: factors of an extra-economic order were all-powerful in the distribution of land. Landed wealth was not accumulated, whatever the level of society, by means of an economic process or by purchase. As a general rule, land was not bought. It was initially inherited; marriage was then the occasion to add to one's property by a skilfully negotiated dowry; finally there was the prospect of benefiting from the generosity of another, that is, from a donation. At the very bottom of the social scale, small allod-holders expanded their patrimonies by bringing into cultivation land belonging to a richer landowner who, at the end of five years, relinquished to them in full ownership one half of the parcel assarted (contract of *méplant*), though this supposed that they would be within his clientèle. At a higher level, there was a reasonable prospect of benefiting from the generosity of the count in the form of a gift (in full ownership) or a benefice (in tenure) in return for services rendered and unwavering loyalty. Conversely, landed fortunes constantly disintegrated under the influence of factors of a similar nature: at marriage, the husband constituted a dower to enable his wife, should the occasion arise, to survive him in decent circumstances; above all, inheritance (practised according to a rule of strict equality, including for daughters) constantly dissolved patrimonies; lastly, the increasingly widespread practice of pious donations reduced them irrevocably.

Disintegration, reintegration: this double movement constantly shuffled individual patrimonies. It was controlled, it is clear, by family structures, by a social factor (the existence of ties of dependence) and by the influence of public institutions (civil and religious). It is easy to imagine how the chances of social preferment, or even of simply holding on to a position within the hierarchy, depended on one's proximity to power. This was one of the causes, perhaps the principal cause, of a phenomenon which will be discussed at some length later, which we will call the 'containing of the economy', in order to emphasise that an economic sphere with real autonomy did not exist. The very powerful determinants of a political, religious and social order prevented this, and consigned the economy to a sort of confinement. A failure to pay careful attention to this phenomenon makes it difficult to understand the functioning of the social system itself. It becomes impossible to perceive the difference in kind which contrasts it with the future feudal system. The proximity of power (the political factor) no doubt always played a role – the rise of the ministers (seigneurial officers) is one illustration – but the relative autonomy of economic factors would increasingly assert itself, making possible the emergence of enriched peasants, not to speak of merchants. Such processes were in the tenth century inconceivable; there was no concentration of land at one pole, and consequently no proletarianisation at the other. The rural society of the Carolingian period did not include, for these reasons, a true layer of marginalised poor, whereas they proliferated under St Louis and Philip the Fair. Most of these rustics lived hard, even very hard, lives, but they all possessed at least something (social marginality was of a political or juridical character, represented by the slaves). Without this basic fact, the stability demonstrated by the small free peasantry, and its ability to resist for so long the pressure of the powerful, would be incomprehensible.

Let us observe, finally, that the situation described was not new in the tenth century. Moses Finley has made the absence of a land market and the regulation of wealth by the political power a central element in his theory of the ancient system.[12] It is true that the state was then at the height of its power and that the Germanic invasions would deal it a hard blow. But the weakness of the state did not interrupt this mode of regulation. In the absence of fiscal resources, the Merovingian and Carolingian kings drew on the public landed reserves (the 'fisc') in order to make distributions which had numerous consequences. They embarked on conquests so as to alleviate the exhaustion of the fisc. The Church, whose hierarchy had become an obvious substitute for the state, participated in this mechanism, taking with one hand, in the form of donations, redistributing with the other, in the form of precarious tenure. In the nature of things, the means changed and became rarer to the extent that the weakness of the state increased. The role of the Church and that of ties of dependence were accordingly enhanced, kinship constrained to a greater vigilance. At the end of the day, the role of extra-economic factors remained equally powerful, consigning the land market to the back burner, to a marginal role – in fact a situation of the ancient type.

The sudden awakening of the land market

But things were perhaps beginning to change. There are several complementary indications, visible under the microscope, which suggest that this might be the case. The first concerns the practice of exchanging land. In a society where the land market was almost non-existent, and where the accidents of inheritance meant lands might be acquired some distance apart or in other territories, the exchange of parcels was a normal procedure – equivalent, on the plane of land, to barter in simple commodities. To analyse this phenomenon, let us classify land transactions into three groups: exchanges, sales and donations (lumping together donations in full ownership and those associated with a precarious reconveyance); let us then calculate the respective percentage of each type of transaction for three successive chronological periods: 920–50, 950–80 and 980–1000. The highly significant result appears in Fig. 1.

Fig. 1 Percentage of sales, exchanges and donations (%)

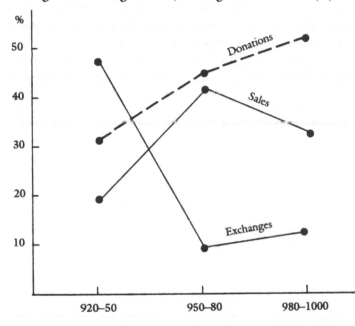

Fig. 1 shows first a very marked discontinuity between 950 and 980, characterised by a sharp drop in exchanges (from 48 per cent to 10 per cent), almost entirely compensated by an increase in sales. It also reveals a steady increase in donations in favour of the abbey, continuing to the end of the century. With respect to these gifts, let us for the moment simply observe that the trend expresses the evolution of power relations in favour of the monks, inasmuch as a donation was not simply an act of piety but also the search for protection when economic or political circumstances turned nasty. The inversion of the exchange/sale relation is surely presumptive evidence of an awakening of the land market. It supposes, in any case, a mental process which was by no means obvious: the monetary expression of the value of a piece of land.

Such a presumption calls for confirmation. It is to be found in an examination of the movement of prices. If a market existed, it ought to be reflected in a certain coherence in the price of land. The difficulty of such an approach is clearly of a technical order. Directly utilisable figures (giving not only the price but the precise area of the land sold) are few and concern different categories of land (curtilages, fields, meadows, vineyards). To avoid merging disparate elements, we will use the fullest series (that of vineyards) and record the price by superficial unit of ten square perches, as in Fig. 2.[13]

Fig. 2   Price of vineyards (in *sous*, in units of ten square perches)

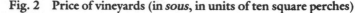

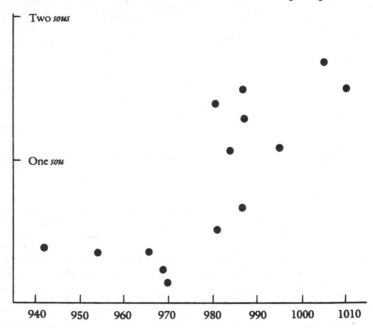

Fig. 2 merits extended discussion. Once again – and in more spectacular fashion than before – the rupture of the years 970–80 is confirmed. The few prices at our disposal for the first two-thirds of the century have such a tenuous relationship to the later prices that it is reasonable to see them as conventional prices, imposed and unrelated to economic reality. There follows a sudden hardening, not to say rocketing, of prices after 970, precisely, that is, when sales of land became frequent. This can only be the irruption of the phenomenon of the market, the sudden pressure of profound economic factors bursting through the carapace of custom which had hitherto frozen the price of land. These were not, of course, pure market prices – an absurd notion, even in a free economy of today. The spread of prices on one or other side of an immediately visible trend clearly points to the action of other factors. A social factor is indeed very clear. In the first period, most of the vendors were from families of modest rank, accepting without jibbing unduly whatever conditions were imposed; the monks penetrated the layer of small allod-holders without difficulty. This was not the case later, when they coveted the lands of the large allod-holders. Round about the year 1000, for example, a certain Arleius, a representative of one of the two chief local lineages, sold a part of his inheritance – two fields, a meadow and a third of a wood – for the sum of seventeen *sous*, of which he received only seven, since he owed the abbey ten *sous*; one can easily imagine the hard bargaining which must have preceded this transaction.[14]

That said, the economic fact remains clear and its effect on the mobility of landed possessions cannot be overestimated. By chance, we have an exceptional deed which can be dated (to within two or three years) to 995 and which provides vivid testimony to the effects of the explosion of the market. The donor, Richelmus, on the point of death, gave away the whole of his property, which he described in detail;[15] it consisted of his inheritance properly speaking (*omnem meam possessionem sive hereditatem*), but also everything he had purchased from, he specified, 'free men', whose names were recorded. Out of a total of nineteen parcels, nine were purchases, all made from small allod-holders. This reveals the extent of the change, and the serious threat it represented for a society of small landowners whose structural stability was suddenly called into question.

It seems likely that the steady increase in donations reflects this situation; better to cede ownership of one's property to the abbey while retaining use of it than lose everything by burning one's fingers in the market. But we should at all cost avoid speaking of a 'new conjuncture', even though it is true that, with the intervention of the economic factor, we are witnessing the birth of the economic conjuncture properly speaking, whose marked long-term movements, typical of the feudal system, would persist up to the eighteenth century. To resort to the cure-all explanation of the conjuncture would be to see only one part of the picture, when in the presence of a much more fundamental change, of a structural order.

Exactly what change, it is at this point too early to say. But one can easily imagine that the sudden mobility of land could only have emerged within a wider economic context; the penetration of money into the furthest reaches of the countryside and the growth of rural trade were its prior conditions. Similarly, we see rural indebtedness become more common, and the shocks caused by subsistence crises were both more frequent and more severe. A new economic atmosphere was displacing the old. We must look beyond its superficial symptoms in our attempt to perceive its character.[16]

For now, let us return to our point of departure. 'A community of status: citizens and landowners': the emphasis was thus put on the connection between the two dimensions of one same reality, the political and the economic; one could not function without the other, and the stability of the allod depended on this combination. Not only was it not threatened by the action of economic factors, which were largely held in check till the middle of the tenth century, but it found in the status of the tree man the necessary protection against the various pressures it faced. It was not easy, even for a powerful personage, to seize the land of a neighbour of lesser condition. The latter retained the possibility of recourse to the courts. We should not see the allod and the condition of the free man as sorts of survival or social residue of little consequence. Both remained central to the social structure, as did slavery (to which they were dialectically linked), as essential elements in its composition.

But the rot had set in. The participation of free men in public institutions now existed only in principle. And their rights over land had suffered two severe blows. The pervasive presence of the monks had led to the conversion of many allods into 'precarious tenures'; above all, the irruption of money and the emergence of a land market had suddenly changed the rules of the game. The various social mechanisms which, over and above the constant but superficial shuffling of patrimonies, had maintained a relative stability and congealed the hierarchies, were revealed as impotent before this strange virus come from outside. The community of status was about to be torn apart. We will see this more clearly as we proceed with our examination of its various constituent parts.

The hierarchy of the free

Georges Lukacs recently observed that in pre-capitalist societies status-consciousness masks class-consciousness.[17] Within a community of status there appears as it were a stack of social strata, separated by barriers which are invisible but yet impassable. How should these groups be described? They had features both of class and caste. Of caste in the sense that their members were to all intents and purposes imprisoned within them, but it was a caste without juridical frontiers, since the only true frontier of this order encompassed all free persons. Of class above all, since the true criterion of differentiation was the relation of these men to the means of production. The classification envisaged is, it must be admitted at the outset, schematic, even arbitrary. The paradox is, in effect, that in spite of the separation described, we find within each of these social categories a spectrum of conditions. Thus it was possible to move by imperceptible transitions from one category to another. Let us accept, however, the risks of schematisation so as to be able to identify the essence, that is the existence of three groups of very unequal size. At the base of the hierarchy was a narrow layer of men who worked the land of others; in the middle was a compact group of peasants properly speaking, cultivating their own land; at the summit of the local pyramid, lastly, were a small number of masters, whom we first glimpsed above through their slaves.

The coloni

The generic term *coloni* designates the bottom layer of free men, lacking a patrimony and compelled to put themselves at the service of men of better birth, or the abbey. They lived on small holdings (a curtilage or a manse) entrusted to them by one of the large allod-holders, and their actual condition was little different from that of the slaves installed on other holdings belonging to the same master. They were not numerous (less than 4 or 5 per cent of the total population), since the norm for masters remained, it will be recalled, the employment of servile labour. But these men, originating in the free community, had lost their footing and were sinking into dependence. A deed of 981 enables us to appreciate their condition and, above all, compare it with that of the slaves.[18] Arleus then granted two manses to the abbey. With the first, he included in his donation a couple of

slaves (Gilbert and his wife) without further details; the second manse
was to be 'held' by a certain Evrardus, 'as long as he lives', in return for
four *setiers* of wine a year, Evrardus thereby becoming a *colonus* of the
abbey. All is made plain in the few lines of a donation. Not a word was
breathed of Evrardus's family; it belonged neither to his master nor to
the abbey. In providing him with a guarantee of life occupancy (of
which there could be no question for a slave), the deed demonstrates
the reality of the rights acquired over the land. Lastly, the charges
weighing on this land were specified, whilst the slave remained subject
to a *servitium* whose imprecise character left the door open to arbitrary
exploitation. Though very close to the slave, the *colonus*, who performed the same labour, probably lived in a fairly similar house and
supported the same master, was nevertheless very different, as long, at
least, as the juridical frontier survived.

Thus, alongside the old servile relationship, even in rivalry with it,
we see appear and develop a new 'relation of production' based on the
system of the tenure, poised to expand and become general. Indeed,
the take-off was already a fact. Year after year, tenures nibbled away at
the area occupied by allods and the number of the abbey's tenants
grew. We know that the abbey had got hold of a good third of the
cultivable area. What mode of exploitation did it choose? For the
tenth century, almost nothing is, in practice, known. The actual
organisation of the seigneurie of Cluny in Lournand and its environs
does not really begin to emerge until after 1010, after, that is, the long
troubled period which saw the birth of the new social system. We have
to wait for the mid twelfth century before it becomes clear how it
functioned, with the classic structure of two elements: seigneurial
demesne and peasant tenures. But it is reasonable to assume that there
had been a continuous process and that this structure had emerged at
an early date. We see the monks systematically acquiring the lands
surrounding the castle of Lourdon, land which would form the
principal element in Cluny's demesne until the eighteenth century. A
part of their land must therefore have been cultivated directly with the
aid of domestic labour, servile or not. The rest was entrusted to
tenants according to the system of 'precarious tenure'. This mode of
land tenure, much employed by the Church, is described in many
deeds. Numerous gifts made by the faithful had as a counterpart a
'precarious' grant back: the donor then became a 'precarious tenant'
(or lessee); he lost the eminent right of ownership, but retained use of

the land. The grant was in principle for life, but in practice soon became hereditary. The precarious tenant had to pay an annual fixed rent for the 'investiture' of the holding. This consisted either of a few pennies (two or four) or, more often, of a certain quantity of wine. It was more a recognition than a real charge, less heavy at all events than those which would later burden tenants once the seigneurie proper had been established.

The condition of the precarious tenants was thus more enviable than that of the private *coloni*, even if their rights and obligations were comparable. Instead of being subject to a private person, some local notable, they were dependent on a collective master who enjoyed considerable prestige. We should not forget that, in an atmosphere dominated by a slave-owning mentality, the simple fact of working for a private person assumed a humiliating character.

Were they numerous? We have to recognise at once that it is impossible to propose figures. The grant of a precarious tenure did not in itself mean a deed was drawn up; this only happened in cases where there was a prior change of ownership. There were certainly precarious tenants unknown to us. Conversely, we should not include in this category allod-holders who held 'precariously' only a small part of their land, the rest being held in full ownership.

What is certain is that this group was gradually being swollen by new recruits consequent upon donations (reassigned precariously). Was this motivated by religious feeling? We have no reason to cast doubt on the sincerity of the sentiments of these men and women, or, even more, on the fears they felt for their salvation. We need only record, through the simple chronology of the deeds, the successive waves of the movement: 959, 963, 974 and above all the terrible years 982, 983 and 984 (the crucial years of this century). Debt and famine were cited. The clauses of the deeds are also revealing. Thus Aynardus of Chevagny, in 964, retaining as a precarious tenure the 'demesne manse' with vineyard and field he had just ceded, specified that the monks ought to provide their support to his young family (*sustineant et beneficiant duos parvulos quod habeo*).[19] And a woman, probably a widow, Aremberta, in 974, making a similar grant of 'a manse with a vineyard and half of what was attached to this curtilage' (*sic*), sought the assistance of the monks until her death.[20] Clearly, whether intended or not, the 'economic' was surfacing, and it is all strangely reminiscent of the scenario simultaneously being enacted in the

Byzantine countryside. But let us not engage in a prolonged and futile debate as to the respective role of material and mental factors. In a period of increasing difficulties, the weaker elements in the social body tended to polarise around a rising star (the abbey) by virtue of tutelage: this was a global fact, whose full significance needs to be appreciated. A social phenomenon, new as a mass phenomenon, suddenly appeared on the horizon in the 980s: downwards social mobility. Its first victims were the small allod-holders.

The peasantry

To define the central group of village (or hamlet) society as 'small allod-holders' is a rough and ready statement which needs to be qualified in at least two ways. The first has already emerged in the previous discussion. Many of these peasant landowners cultivating their own land also held one or more parcels from the abbey by precarious tenure, so that the frontier between tenants and allod-holders is difficult to establish; it often passed through the individual himself. Nor should we assume a homogeneous economic condition. By this period, another frontier separated those whose holdings were sufficiently large for them to possess a plough team (they would soon be called *laboureurs*) and those who were unable to keep draught animals (oxen) and had no other tools than the spade and the hoe (the *manouvriers*). These words, and consequently this distinction, probably never appear in tenth-century documents, for the simple reason that juridical definitions took precedence over all other considerations. But once slavery had disappeared from the scene, the economic distinction emerged into the light of day. An extract from the cartulary of Saint-Vincent of Mâcon, dating from the mid eleventh century, illustrates this perfectly: Guichard of Beaujeu renounced various 'bad customs' levied on the 'villeins' (*villani*), except those demanded for their protection (*salvamentum*), namely a *setier* of grain from those who worked with oxen, and a half *setier* from the poor (*pauperiores*) who, it was spelt out, worked manually in the vineyards with hoes (*cum fossoribus*).[21] The revival of trade had by that date probably deepened, though it had not created, the gulf between these two groups. Its origins were ancient and derived in part at least from the progress of agricultural equipment (the increase in the size of the plough team), a slow evolution if ever there was one. We need to bear this in mind for the tenth century and appreciate that this distinction further complicated social relations. A *manouvrier* was by definition economically dependent; his holding was too small to assure the subsistence of his family. Work as a craftsman sometimes brought him additional resources, but he was often obliged to work for a *laboureur* or large allod-holder, in particular at times of peak seasonal demand for labour. Such relations of dependence restricted the autonomy of a sector, perhaps the major sector, of the allod-holders.

This group nevertheless played a central role, which made it indispensable to the stability of the social body as a whole, in the first place by its numerical importance. There is a risk, it is true, of overestimating their number inasmuch as the sources favour landowners. But we have allowed for this by making a generous estimate of the under-represented social groups (slaves and *coloni*).[22] Overall, the order of magnitude during the course of the tenth century was close to 60 per cent of the total population, though with an uneven geographical distribution. They were present in large numbers in the hamlet of Lournand, where slaves and large allod-holders were rare. We see here a disconcerting historical continuity; the particular physiognomy of Lournand, land par excellence of small cultivators and wine-producers in the early modern period and today, was already strongly marked in the tenth century. Such men were less numerous at Chevagny and Collonge, and the percentage declines sharply as soon as we leave the hills and their light soils for the Grosne valley.[23]

As well as being numerically dominant, the small allod-holders also accounted for a majority of the cultivated area. Using the same method as that used to estimate the proportion of Church and private land (deduced from the boundaries), we can estimate very roughly that the small allod-holders held about two-thirds of the latter (that is, more than 40 per cent of the whole), the final third being in the hands of a few rich families. To this must be added the by no means negligible amount of Church land held by precarious tenure. Overall, the major share of production rested on the shoulders of these peasant-wineproducers, backbone of the rural economy.

They formed, in fact, the most stable, the most solidly entrenched and the most coherent element in village society. Below them, neither the slaves nor the *coloni* had the same reasons to demonstrate their attachment to a territorial unit or community. Above them, the large allod-holders had wider horizons which distanced them from the hamlet and made them prefer a military or clerical way of life. These peasants, then, were the transmitters of historical continuity. They showed proof of this some centuries later, when the area experienced the hell of the end of the Middle Ages, followed by the Wars of Religion; the old territories of the small peasantry survived the shock, whereas Merzé and Cotte were deserted and never recovered.

But as allod-holders, these peasants were under threat. They were threatened first – though this was not new – by the small number of large allod-holders, to be discussed later, who dominated the local horizon. To illustrate the contradiction opposing them, let us employ a geometrical metaphor: the social configuration was triangular. Thanks to their possession of a certain landed wealth and, above all, slaves (the one, obviously, dependent on the other), the masters enjoyed a hegemonic social position from which they benefited vis-à-vis the peasantry proper by using this domination to exploit it in various ways. The relation between them has perhaps too readily been seen in strictly landed terms, as if the masters must have been tempted to seize for themselves the patrimonies of the small allod-holders. There is no evidence to suggest this in the sources. It is highly probable that the few men described as 'free', but installed on a curtilage or manse belonging to a master, were former small land-owners (or their descendants) who, one fine day, had seen no alternative but to place themselves under the protection of a master, in a manner resembling the old Merovingian *commendatio*, and had then surrendered their property. But this process, we repeat, seems never to have assumed the character of a mass movement, for which the persistence of slavery is sufficient explanation. Taking it all in all, an efficient functioning of the social triangle was a solution satisfactory to the masters, and they well understood that it was in their interests to have around them peasant communities which were alive rather than dying.

The evidence suggests that they profited from their mills (already constructed throughout the Mâconnais by the beginning of the tenth century).[24] They often owned woods adjoining those of the communities, and it is reasonable to suppose that they allowed certain activities in them in return for services or rents. They also established ties of clientage among the small allod-holders, such as those benefiting from contracts of *méplant*. One can understand why, in these circumstances, André Deléage and Georges Duby spoke of them as 'small lords' and 'small lordships'. I would be entirely happy to accept the use of these terms if they did not have the disadvantage of concealing the persistence of the servile relationship which supported the nascent seigneurial relationship. 'Embryonic lordships' is perhaps a better term – embryos of which very few reached full term, or where, to put it another way, the small lord gradually broke through the skin of the master. In any case, from this relation of exploitation derived a latent contradiction between masters and small allod-holders.

It seems – and this was something new – that the contradiction deepened, especially in the two last decades of the century. The most obvious sign is the now explicit affirmation of the 'customs' claimed by these local 'squireens'. When, in 1005, Eldinus granted his inheritance in Cotte comprising a piece of forest, he saw fit to mention the custom attached to it and that he held 'like the other nobles' (*sicut alii nobiles*).[25] A similar claim was made by Bernard, brother of Achard (a member of the most powerful family in the *ager* of Merzé): he enjoyed, he said, *consuetudines* in many territories.[26] Another sign is the acquisition at this same period of parish churches with all their revenues, especially tithes.[27] The church of Lournand was among them, granted by the bishop to the two brothers of Ornadus. All this is indicative of the desire to establish a direct domination over the ancient peasant communities.

That the small allod-holders were the chief victims is not in doubt. Increased pressure certainly served to unsettle further a social group already deeply shaken by the new economic atmosphere (notably the emergence of the land market), perhaps also by some fragmentation of their patrimonies thanks to the demographic conjuncture. From mid century, the signs of impoverishment multiply. Indebtedness with the mortgaging of land was the first step in a downward social progress. The next was easily predictable. We do not know the fate of the couple of allod-holders of Lournand who mortgaged their curtilage with a meadow and vineyard for a loan of nine *sous*, repayable in four years; they simply disappear from our sources, as do the two sons whose names were recorded in the deed.[28] We should perhaps see in the rising trend of donations in favour of Cluny (many of them leased back) the result as much as the cause of peasant poverty, as if a sort of forward retreat enabled them to hope not only for eternal salvation but for the assistance of the monks, less distressing, all things considered, than that of their importunate neighbours.

It seems that the triangular structure described above gradually functioned less efficiently. The domination of the masters over the slaves, let us not forget, became less sure. They were then tempted, if not constrained, to widen the scope of their exploitation, at the risk of destabilising the pivotal group in society. The two social contradictions were probably closely linked: the deeper one (masters/slaves) propelling the second (masters/small allod-holders) on to the forefront of the stage.

The masters

The masters have frequently made an appearance in the previous pages; it is now time to examine them more closely. The sources for the masters are better than for the small allod-holders. The explanation is very simple; when one of them concluded a transaction, his family, immediate (his descendants) or less close (cousins or brothers-in-law), recorded their agreement and therefore appear in the deed, often with an indication of the relationship. This specific circumstance makes it possible to lift a corner of the veil which normally obscures family and relationships; since the abandonment of the Roman system of personal naming, each individual bore, in effect, one name and one only, generally unrelated to that of his parents. It was not until the twelfth century that there appeared a surname which rapidly became the family name.[29] Before this happened, it is impossible to reconstitute the family molecules on the basis of the individual atoms, and family structures remain shrouded in an almost impenetrable mist. The information at our disposal concerning the masters makes it possible to some degree to circumvent this obstacle and above all to gain a clearer understanding of this social group, and trace with greater precision its contours and the networks which structure it. We have therefore sketched out the genealogies of the seven families of masters who dominated the *ager* of Merzé, designating each one by the name of the central person (in one case, it was necessary to use two names), that is the person who seems to have played the most active role in the last two decades of the century.[30] They are: Achard–Bernard (Achardus–Bernardus) at Merzé; Arlier (Arleus or Arleius) at Merzé and Collonge; Seguin (Seguinus) at Varanges; Engelelm (Engelelmus) at Varanges; Anselard (Anselardus) at Cotte; Elduin (Eldinus) at Cotte; Ademar at Varanges.

In relation to the total population of the *ager*, these families, some of which included several married couples, represented an element which is difficult to measure but which was by no means negligible (perhaps of the order of 6 or 7 per cent); at all events, the masters were significantly more numerous than the nobles would later be within feudal society. Belonging to the same community of status as the other free persons, subject to the same obligations and the same rights, they were in no way distinguished in the texts, except by an occasional *quidam vir*, implying a certain esteem. We have to wait until the years 985–90 to see some of them dignified by the title of *nobilis* or *miles*. A page had then been turned. For the moment, they were distinguished from ordinary allod-holders by three simple criteria, which we will now examine.

The first and most obvious concerns their patrimonies, composed of lands and men (the slaves). The most modest of them, Anselard and Elduin, had at least three or four small exploitations worked by *servi* or, occasionally, by a *colonus*; they also owned woods or parts of woods. The richest of them (Achard–Bernard or Arlier) owned as many as ten manses or curtilages, some situated outside the *ager* of Merzé, in one of the neighbouring villages such as Massilly or Flagy. This implies neither large areas (at most, thirty to forty hectares of cultivable land) nor compact estates. It was rather a question of clusters of small exploitations scattered over several territories, and in amongst those of the peasantry; these clusters were, furthermore, constantly being shuffled by inheritance and land transactions, especially exchanges. But all these small estates (or embryonic landed lordships), without exception, had a sort of central nucleus in the Grosne valley, close to the vast forested zone separating Merzé and Cotte from Varanges. Most of this woodland, with the exception of a fraction of the wood of Cotte, belonged to the masters. We will return, in the next chapter devoted to an economic analysis, to the implications of this fact, especially as regards the pastoral orientation of their activities. For the moment, let us simply emphasise the social contrast. On the one hand, on the limestone hills, peasant-wineproducers with few animals; here, much richer men, disposing of meadows, large stretches of woodland and abundant livestock – pigs, of course, but also cattle and goats. It is not difficult to guess that hunting was their daily sport and war already their dominant social function.

Their property, it should be stressed, was allodial; it was held neither of the count nor of one of the four or five great aristocratic families of the Mâconnais. It might have been received as a gift, a century or two earlier, on the initiative of the Carolingians, intent on 'holding' in some sense the region; or they might simply have been the remote descendants of the Frankish men of war who settled there at the time of the conquest. It is impossible to say. The second hypothesis would coincide perfectly with the geography of Germanic settlement outlined by Henri Gaillard de Sémainville on the basis of a study of barbarian cemeteries in the Grosne valley;[31] in which case, this would be the most advanced front of this wave of settlement. This hypothesis, if it could be verified (but how?), would upset several received ideas regarding the rapid fusion of the two elements, Germanic and Gallo-Roman.

The second distinguishing criterion was a matter of family structure. When a simple allod-holder alienated a property, only he and his wife, as a general rule, were involved in the act; the narrow family wholly owned the property in question. In the case of one of the masters, the family manifested its presence and approved the donation. Thus Achard in 995, on the approach of death, confirmed an earlier donation comprising several pieces of land and a wood.[32] The donation was approved by his three sons, his first cousin on his mother's side, a 'relation' (*propinquus*), his daughter and his son-in-law. This may reveal an extended family, contrasting with the narrow family, the overwhelmingly predominant model among the surrounding peasantry; in which case, it is possibly a late survival of the Germanic *Sippe*. One thing at least is sure, and that is the crucial importance of marriage alliances for this social group, and the solidarity which resulted. The study of our seven families of the *ager* of Merzé reveals a tightly-knit network uniting them to each other and to families of comparable rank in the neighbouring villages. Engelelm of Varanges was *consanguinus* of Arlier; Hugo, brother of Elduin, became the son-in-law of Achard when he married his daughter, Roselina; Eva, sister of Anselard, became the wife of Arlier; Ademar was cousin both to Achard and Bernard and to Arlier, and so on. Matrimonial strategies responded to the primeval preoccupation with maintaining the family patrimony in a society where inheritance regulated the circulation of land. No marriage, accordingly, was made outside the social level of the masters.

But to have allies and family, of the highest possible rank, responded to another, and an equally essential, need: the combining of forces to improve opportunities to approach the power which dispensed honours and revenues. Georges Duby has produced penetrating analyses of the evolution of aristocratic family structures. He has shown how a new structure of kinship was formed in the eleventh century, 'based on the agnatic relationship and of vertical orientation', in which the individual felt himself to be a 'member of a lineage, of a stock, where, from father to son, a heritage was transmitted'.[33] This was a decisive break with the earlier situation. 'Previously', he wrote,

there was no lineage, no properly genealogical awareness, no coherent memory of one's ancestors; a man from the aristocracy saw his family as, if I may use the expression, a horizontal group, extending in the present, as a group with imprecise and shifting boundaries, composed as much of *propinqui* as of *consanguinei*, of men and women linked to him as much by blood as by the consequences of matrimonial alliances. What counted for him and his fortunes was less his ancestors than his 'nearest', through whom he approached power . . . politically, he looked to a prince for everything: what mattered to him was his relations, not his ancestors.

These words are equally valid for the small group we are studying. A barely nascent consciousness of lineage is visible in only two families, in their adoption of the practice of giving one child in each new generation the name of Bernard or Achard in the one case, Arlier in the other, names already carrying a certain prestige. But the real issue for these families remained their relation to power, that is their access to the prevailing political and religious structures: to approach, that is, as close as possible to the count or the bishop. This was crucial, since partition through inheritance was constantly breaking up patrimonies. In the absence of such a close relationship to these structures, the reproduction of their social hegemony became impossible. In this sense, the fate of the group was historically linked to that of the Carolingian institutions, and the political (in the wide sense: I include, of course, the ecclesiastical structures), weak though it was, continued to put its mark on the social by making possible the perpetuation of the hierarchies. This is why the decline of the state condemned this social stratum, as such, to extinction. Only some of its members would survive the wreck, enabling their lineage, finally affirmed, to insert itself into a strong position in a new social order, at the cost of a dramatic transformation.

The third criterion differentiating the masters from the free peasantry was thus political, that is access to various levels of power, as a source of revenues, family structures being the necessary tool to the success of such a quest. The power in question was not local power. Georges Duby has argued strongly against the idea that 'the powers of command derived from the prerogatives of the lord of land'.[34] Direct authority was exercised by the masters over their slaves alone by right of ownership. As regards free men, they enjoyed only those advantages procured by economic pre-eminence; real authority, the power to constrain, proceeded from the public institutions and from them alone, that is, in the first instance, from Mâcon.

It was thus towards Mâcon that their eyes were turned. What might they expect? From the count, not much; the grant of 'benefices' to the 'loyal' was rare in the case of these modest local squireens, and only a few large families benefited in the Mâconnais. But they had high hopes of the Church, in the first place because of its landed wealth, constantly being enlarged by the pious donations which made possible grants of land in precarious tenure, and because, above all, of its revenues: from its estates, from various offerings and from tithe. In a society where direct fiscality had collapsed in the sixth century, the ecclesiastical hierarchy, among other functions, constituted an ersatz fiscal machine. In a sense, the tithe had resuscitated the ancient land tax. It was principally by this channel that the free peasantry (in appearances not subject to a relation of exploitation) had to participate in the maintenance of the upper ranks of society. The social redistribution of the revenue thus levied (that is significantly more than 10 per cent of gross agricultural produce) was effected through the intermediary of the clerical hierarchy. By the same token, the recruitment of the clergy, and their progress through the various stages of the secular hierarchy, were crucial issues.

There can be little doubt that it was the masters who received the largest slice of the cake. The simple allod-holders had to make do with the crumbs. They provided the 'Levites', clerics confined to minor posts, often economic in nature. A few acceded to the priesthood, such as the Eldradus of Merzé, who, it has been suggested, should be ranked with simple allod-holders (since among his property, albeit modest, figured a piece of land acquired thanks to a contract of *méplant* made with Arlier), but who was very close to the dominant social stratum (he owned a slave granted to Cluny in 991).[35] In practice, the ecclesiastical structures were essentially an apanage of the masters. Mainbodus, bishop of Mâcon in the mid tenth century, was a typical representative of this social stratum;[36] born in the neighbouring territory of Ruffey (a hamlet which disappeared very early as a result of the growth of the agglomeration of Cluny), where his family had been settled for several generations, he possessed several manses or curtilages and some slaves. None of our masters from the *ager* of Merzé enjoyed such a brilliant career. Neverthless, in the tenth century alone, Sendelenus was an archdeacon (he was the brother of Engelelm, who himself became a priest); Achard, brother of Bernard, was a *clericus* in the evening of his life; the family of Arlier also counted many priests; Anselard of Cotte was a 'Levite'. In sum, the ecclesiastical career was the normal route for one, if not several, male children of each generation, and it is difficult to see how this group could have retained its position without this indispensable support. Their landed wealth, their servile capital and their social pre-eminence should not blind us to the economic difficulties with which they struggled. Arlier, as we saw above, was heavily in debt to the monks. It is highly significant that, by the 950s, a tense atmosphere had developed between the monastery and these local notables.

The worst possible outcome for them would have been for the umbilical cord attaching them to Mâcon to be cut. There lay the most serious risk of downward social mobility, and it loomed increasingly large in the second half of the tenth century. In the interminable process of the decline of the state (or public institutions), a new and final stage was beginning, visible in a sort of carving up of the *pagus* of Mâcon, here under the influence of Cluny, elsewhere under that of the powerful families of castellans. It broke into pieces this sort of superior political society, of which the masters were the only members, and threatened their existence as a social group. Proof that this was a vital issue for them was to be provided not only by the violence of their reactions but even more by the preferred objective they set themselves, that is to get their hands on the local churches and their revenues; in other words, so as to remain in the fiscal register, to make a 'deduction at source'.

We will examine later (for it is one of the main themes of the progress towards the feudal revolution) the process which remodelled the upper category of free men, propelling some on the path to downwards social mobility, others to social promotion by the acquisition of a new social identity (knighthood).[37] For the moment, let us note only that it cannot be dissociated from the political and that to study it supposes a prior approach to the structural framework.

Where the political structures the social

We must be careful, firstly, not to see in the structural framework a sort of distinct 'instance' or 'superstructure' placed on or laid over the social field, as if its sole function was to contain the contradictions. They were, and this will be our guiding notion, constituent elements of the social order. This was, as we have seen, characterised by a strict hierarchy. If we ignore for the moment the 'free' *coloni* (a transitory product of social decline affecting the peasantry), three levels emerge: the slaves, the peasants and the masters. The accident of birth determined the distribution of the population between these three groups: heredity in law for the division between free and non-free; heredity in fact for that between the free categories.

This is a classification which can be read in two ways. The first and most obvious reading is in terms of class. It was a structure with three classes, not two: men who owned nothing, not even their labour power, which belonged to others; peasants owning their means of production but subject to exploitation of, in the last analysis, a fiscal nature; and masters living off servile labour and consequently enjoying a hegemony from which they profited by a second set of levies, of an indirect type.

But to be satisfied with this reading alone proceeds from an unfortunate reductionism, since the juridical and political elements are inextricably interwoven in the structuring of the economic order. Here, too, there emerges a ternary arrangement, produced by the combination of two binary systems. In one, the free as a group, belonging to one same community of status, were opposed to the slaves, who were excluded, according to the constitutive principle of the political organisation of 'ancient' societies. The other divided the community of the free into two sub-groups, ranked not only by their respective levels of wealth but also by a political criterion which was no less real for being less obvious. Each group was in practice firmly confined within its original category, as if they were orders, by extra-economic factors: a specific structural framework, sufficiently active for the 'political' to be able to freeze the hierarchies. In other words, social relations were maintained within a political envelope, a sort of corset, which gave coherence to what we will now call a 'social system', in order to emphasise more strongly the interdependence of its elements.

Our discussion of these structures will be brief, since our local approach adds nothing to the admirable analysis provided by Georges Duby.[38] We will be content to accept his conclusions with regard to the two questions which concern us here: in what way did the distribution of power (that is the state) structure the social? And how did this distribution develop?

Horizontal partition

The basic context was the county of Mâcon, a territory correspond-ing, roughly speaking, to the contemporary department of Saône-et-Loire without the Chalonnais, but extending westwards as far as the Loire. Since the Partition of Verdun (843), it had been part of the kingdom of western Francia. Royal power, however, was too far distant for it any longer really to make itself felt. The county of Mâcon was thus a sort of autonomous principality held by a sovereign dynasty, a striking illustration of an evolution common to the whole Carolingian world.

In theory, the whole of the free population (the Frankish people) participated in the public life of the county; they were liable to military service (host) and court attendance; their conflicts were the business of the comital court (the *mallum publicum*), keystone of Carolingian institutions. For all free men, there was one leader, the count; such was the political and ideological cement binding in a single whole the community of status, over and above the diversity of its members.

But, looked at more closely, the institutions played a role in the social stratification by establishing a watertight partition between the two categories, upper and lower, of free men. In practice, only the masters were answerable to Mâcon. As regards military obligations, an area about which we have, at the local level, no precise information, it is difficult to say who responded to the summons of the count, through the intermediary of the few great personages to whom custody of the five or six public fortresses controlling the Mâconnais had been entrusted (one of which was the castle of Lourdon, in the hands of the monks). The general dispositions made by Charlemagne in his capitularies of 807 and 808 extended the obligation to serve, previously reserved to those holding at least four manses, to small and middling proprietors, who were asked to band together to send one of them to the host. It is not clear to what extent these dispositions were applied. They were a response to an exceptional military conjuncture. Above all, they came up against both the social evolution (the impoverishment of allod-holders no longer able to support the military burden) and the development of military technique (favouring heavier weapons and the role of men on horseback). In these circumstances, the field of recruitment of fighting men contracted, the principal burden falling, it would appear, on the social stratum of the masters, who formed a sort of mounted militia. From the rest, all that could be required were secondary contributions of a very local character: requisitions in labour to strengthen the walls of the castle of Lourdon or the service of watch. In the judicial domain, the social gulf was even deeper and appeared with considerable clarity. The comital court (which still sat in Mâcon) had as its justiciables only the stratum of the masters. Presided over by the count (sometimes by the bishop) surrounded by the members of the high aristocracy of the county, it appeared as a superior court, in the social sense of the word, attendance restricted to only an elite among the free.

But we should not conclude that the mass of free men were actively excluded from public activity. For those of modest condition, this took place within restricted judicial circumscriptions, the *vigueries* (designated by the terms *ager* or *vicaria*). No document throws much light on the court corresponding to the *ager* of Merzé,[39] but we do have information about the functioning of neighbouring *vigueries*, in particular that of Jalogny.[40] The class character of the institution is crystal clear; the masters did not attend. The vicar (nominated by the count) who presided, the *scabini* or 'good men' who assisted and, lastly, the justiciables, were all of modest condition. The peasants of the various hamlets of the *ager* assembled there. Chief among its activities were cases concerning property, but its competence probably extended to all civil actions, even the most important. In sum, it reproduced, on a restricted scale and for the exclusive use of the peasantry, the court of the count. We referred earlier to the extraordinary resistance manifested up to the tenth century by the peasant allod; this would have been inconceivable but for the enduring vitality of the local courts, where every free man had the right to make his voice heard.

Furthermore, in the community of the hamlet, the peasants possessed a structural framework of their own (not of the state), of a type to strengthen their cohesion. This was a silent and customary community par excellence, its presence signalled only by the existence of the 'common lands' belonging to Lournand, Chevagny and Collonge. It has sometimes been argued that the rural community was a purely medieval creation, consequent upon the establishment of the seigneurial system and the regrouping of population which it brought about. It is probably the case that, from the eleventh century, the social function of the rural community took new forms, a broader dimension, a larger social presence within a changed environment. But this should not cause us to forget the existence of more ancient communities, sufficiently entrenched to have preserved their identity to our own day, as remarked above. On them probably devolved functions of a technical and economic order, obscure, admittedly, but essential to daily existence: the management of the common woods and meadows, the upkeep of the roads designated 'public' and perhaps certain forms of co-operation between its members.

This was how power was distributed in the tenth century. Let us leave Georges Duby to conclude:

> The administration of justice was, in the tenth century, divided between superimposed but watertight compartments, whose disposition corresponded to the main lines of the social edifice: the justice of the master over the *servi*, of the local vicarial assemblies over the lower class of free men, of the comital *mallum* over the great men of the county. In the eleventh century, this superimposition had made way for a geographical juxtaposition.[41]

Towards vertical divisions

The vertical division of the county into a number of territorial units based on a castle or a great monastery, which assumed the power of command and exercised it over the whole population of the surrounding district, was in fact the major event of the beginning of the eleventh century, the political expression of the feudal revolution. It would sweep away within a few years the Carolingian political edifice, tearing open the envelope which had till then maintained the major social forms. The substitution of private authorities for the public authority of the count emptied of all content the 'citizenship' of the free, so destroying the principal frontier behind which slaves avid for integration already massed. In the same way, the subjection of the two categories of free men to the same authority, direct and close at hand, did away with the distinguishing institutional criterion, and deprived of their safety-net the masters threatened with social decline. Inter-dependent in their common existence for centuries, the social struc-tures and the political structures would be together in defeat.

But for the moment, that is up to the 980s, this stage had not yet been reached. The ancient political edifice remained in place – an increasingly fragile edifice in which cracks were proliferating. In the area of our study, they resulted from the emergence of the jurisdiction of the abbey. This had been germinating since the foundation of the abbey as a result of the many guarantees it enjoyed. In 955 it was formally confirmed by a diploma of King Lothair which protected the monks from any judicial intervention.[42] From then on, it extended around Cluny, and especially in the *ager* of Merzé. It is not clear whether it initially applied only to dependents of the abbey or to all the inhabitants of the territory; in the final analysis it matters little, since an ever growing number of former allod-holders and even masters (Arleus, for example) became lessees of the abbey and passed under its jurisdiction. The ancient judicial assembly of the *ager* may have survived for a while, but it was doomed and soon gave way to justice exercised directly by the abbatial deans. The process was com-pleted in the first two decades of the eleventh century, the period when the comital court lost its official and superior character to merge with the other private courts of the county. For the former masters, who had also lost their slaves in the turmoil, the road to Mâcon was cut.

We have now come to the end of our social analysis. It is clearly too early to advance an overall hypothesis when many aspects – notably economic – have not yet been tackled. But, on the basis of our first findings, let us try to draw a few conclusions, though provisional.

The first questions the traditional view of Carolingian society, a society always presented as pre-feudal, inhabited by 'lords' and 'serfs', slipping by imperceptible degrees towards feudal society proper, without any discontinuity or sudden change. The last stages were purely political: the dissolution of the public institutions in favour of a new political system based on personal ties, vassalage and the fief, Such a view places too much emphasis on the history of the 'great' or the rulers, at the expense of the deep social fabric. It also pays too much attention to impressions or to an atmosphere which, it is true, represents a break with that of classical antiquity: a pervasive rurality, the rise of ties of dependence, the penetration of Christianity throughout the whole of social and political life. But it is, finally, belied by the three conclusions which we have reached by the end of our examination of our chosen society.

Firstly, we observe a social structure with three poles, since based on the complex disposition of three classes: the masters, the peasants and the slaves. Such a structure was by no means new in the tenth century. That of Frankish society in the reign of Dagobert, for example, was not significantly different. Further, the fundamental principles of the social edifice, as regards work, ownership and participation in public life, remained wholly in line with those principles which had structured ancient society. To assert this continuity does not imply any denial of the changes which had taken place since the fifth century. It is certainly true that the ambience and social atmosphere were no longer the same. The physiognomy of the actors had changed; the aristocracy had been militarised, the slaves Christianised, the peasantry liberated from the fiscal yoke, and now a more dynamic partner. The relations between the principal actors had also changed; the contradiction between masters and peasants had manifestly deepened as a result of the deficiencies of the state which had formerly primarily served the needs of the dominant class. That said, the disposition of the classes inherited from antiquity had essentially survived. This is surely obvious.

Secondly, the stability of society (in other words, the regular 'reproduction' of its internal hierarchies) was closely linked to the political functioning of the Frankish world. The crisis of the state, a process long under way, thus had as an ineluctable consequence a weakening of the social edifice. It tended to blur the frontier between free and non-free, and deprive the masters of an indispensable support. In brief, the political structured or supported the social increasingly less firmly.

Thirdly, social stability was in the end threatened by new phenomena arising in the economic sphere. Society had long enjoyed a sort of immunity with regard to economic phenomena. Sufficient attention has perhaps not been paid to this simple fact. The absence of a true market (particularly a land market) in the rural economy had been the strongest factor for permanence and social cohesion that it is possible to imagine. It prevented any process of polarisation. The revival of trade, the sudden appearance of large quantities of silver, the mobility of land and the speculation by all orders which followed from it were all destabilising factors. The economic and demographic growth, to the extent that it promoted the impoverishment of peasants and masters, acted in the same sense. For many members of one or other group, the time of downwards social mobility had suddenly arrived; masters had to renounce their idle lifestyle, peasants were obliged to work for others. No phenomenon, perhaps, is more dangerous to the cohesion of a society than social decline which becomes generalised. How could the old structure, its three poles already eroded and weakened, its political supports themselves tottering, tolerate such a shock? It did not do so. But before observing this ultimate ordeal, we should attempt a more precise economic analysis.

Notes

1 The concept of 'ancient society' is used here in the sense given it by Moses Finley.
2 On this point, the best synthesis remains that of Robert Boutruche, *Seigneurie et féodalité*, 2 vols, Paris, 1968.
3 C. C. 606.
4 C. C. 606.
5 Deléage, *Vie rurale en Bourgogne*, pp. 226ff.
6 Duby, *La Société . . . dans la région mâconnaise*, p. 73.
7 This is based on the assumption that the number of private owners mentioned in all the confines correlates more or less with the relative importance of that sector of ownership; and that the same applies to Church lands.
8 They have not been included in Table 1 so as to avoid lumping together the cultivated area of the territorial units and their wooded peripheries. See C. C. 109, 461, 947, 988, 2211, 2334, 2340, 2429, 2556, 2625, 2775.
9 C. C. 2531.
10 C. C. 2845.
11 Duby, *La Société . . . dans la région mâconnaise*, pp. 61ff.
12 Finley, *Ancient Economy*, especially pp. 157–61.
13 I willingly leave aside, for the moment, the irritating problem posed by the length of the perch; I will return to the issue of the weather in a later work devoted to the feudal period.
14 C. C. 2144.
15 C. C. 2136. Date established on the basis of the names of the subscribers at the bottom of the act.
16 See, on this problem, Guy Bois, *Crise du féodalisme*, Paris, 1976 (translated as *The Crisis of Feudalism*, Cambridge, 1984).
17 Georges Lukacs, *Histoire et conscience de class*, Paris, 1960, p. 78 (translated as *History and Class Consciousness*, London, 1971).

18 C. C. 1580.
19 C. C. 1172.
20 C. C. 1391.
21 Cartulaire de Saint-Vincent de Mâcon, 476.
22 For the quantitative aspect of the problem, see Chapter 4, which includes a demographic analysis.
23 Lucien Champier has already emphasised the contrast between the old villages nestling in the hills and the more recent hamlets situated in the valleys which had been colonised by the Romans. See 'Recherches sur les origines du terroir et de l'habitat en Mâconais et Châlonnais', *Etudes rhodaniennes*, 1947.
24 See Chapter 4.
25 C. C. 2621
26 C. C. 2022.
27 Cartulaire de Saint-Vincent de Mâcon, 392.
28 C. C. 848; the sum of nine *sous* was then equivalent to the price of a small rural exploitation.
29 This naming revolution is also significant with regard to the underlying social revolution or advent of the feudal system; it expressed the new solid establishment of lineages, whatever the social level, on the land which was that of their ancestors and which would be transmitted to their descendants. It cannot be said too often: feudalism was based on the peasant family being firmly entrenched on the land of its ancestors.
30 See Appendix.
31 Henri Gaillard de Sémainville, 'Les cimetières mérovingiens de la côte mâconnaise', *Revue archéologique de l'Est et du Centre-Est*, 3rd supplement, Dijon, 1980, pp. 174–80.
32 C. C. 2026.
33 Georges Duby, 'Structures familiales dans le Moyen Age occidental', *XIIe Congrès international des sciences historiques*, Moscow, 1970, reprinted in *Mâle Moyen Age*, Paris, 1988, pp. 144–5.
34 Duby, *La Société . . . dans la région mâconnais*, pp. 83–4.
35 C. C. 1783, 1883. It is not impossible that he was related to Arlier; in which case this would be an example of an impoverished branch of a family of masters.
36 C. C. 667. In exchange for an orchard, he granted to Cluny the curtilage where his father (Otardus) lived and the curtilage where his grandfather lived. So he was clearly not from the high aristocracy.
37 See Chapter 4.
38 In his thesis and, above all, in 'Recherches sur l'évolution du système judicaire pendant le Xe et le XIe siècles dans le sud de la Bourgogne', *Le Moyen Age*, 1946, reprinted in *Hommes et structures du Moyen Age*, 1973.
39 Except, perhaps, the fleeting reference to a *scabinus* called Sievertus, from Collonge and of modest social condition. C. C. 1273 (deed of 969).
40 This village adjoins Cluny to the south.
41 Duby, 'Recherches sur l'évolution du système judiciare', p. 31.
42 C. C. 980.

3
Trade: the birth of the market and a new relationship between town and country

So far, the economy has been left aside, appearing only incidentally, in connection, for example, with the first stages of a land market, whose origins have also not yet been discussed. The priority thereby given to the social has been deliberate. It is predicated on the assumption (already posited) of a sort of 'containing' of the economy within the political and social structure. It seemed of paramount importance to clarify at the outset certain points of social history (the slave base, the tripartite character of the social structure) seen as essential pre-requisites to an understanding of what followed. However, we now come to the economy.

The word, as is well known, satisfies no one. It is dangerous because of the illusion it conveys, that of a clearly circumscribed terrain or of a more or less autonomous sphere. I repeat: there is no such thing (especially in ancient times) as an economy in isolation; each act which is apparently economic is equally cultural or social (for example, the gift). These reservations apart, the term remains useful to indicate a group of activities indispensable to all social life: production (and its extension, 'reproduction'), exchange, the distribution of the product and consumption. What confusion surrounds these terms! Whatever the interactions with other human activities, it is inevitable that regulators will operate between the various parameters. The most archaic of societies is subject to constraints of a macro-economic or micro-economic order: on the one hand, it could not for long con-sume more than it produced, on the other, each unit of production has to come to terms with the requirement for reproduction, sometimes in highly complex ways. Some of these regulators may have a general character and be found in different social systems. But most of them, the evidence suggests, are very clearly specific to each social system – something which historians need constantly to bear in mind if they wish to avoid anachronism and error. Nothing could be more absurd than to place on the same plane the history of prices in the twentieth and the tenth centuries, given that the mechanism by which prices were determined has nothing in common in the two cases. The principal aim of economic history should be to discover the internal regulators, those hidden and obscure mechanisms, which have never ceased – even today – to surprise the most well-informed observers.

Why rehearse such hackneyed banalities? Quite simply, and not to mince words, because the dominant historiography ignores, or pretends to ignore, these manifest truths. It fails to recognise, or prefers not to recognise, the very notion of a socio-economic system. The rest follows; it condemns itself to a general economic history, detached from the underlying systems. This would be by no means without value if it at least remained conscious of its limitations and stuck strictly to a descriptive approach. After all, one can in that strain perfectly well describe the modalities, the chronology and the extent of medieval growth. But to explain it is another matter. A refusal to penetrate the economic specificity of the feudal system entails, by the same token, a refusal to understand the mainsprings of its growth. There follows a cruel alternative: either to recognise this and renounce all interpretation (but how, in that case, justify the exercise?) or dissimulate, by slipping in an explanation, more or less surreptitiously, in order to give some semblance of rationality to the project. In the case of the growth of Europe, demography is usually solicited to this end, as if it goes without saying, as if it was written in tablets of stone, that an increase in the number of people was sufficient to produce a powerful process of growth.

Rejecting such an approach to economic history, we will assume, as our conceptual background, the global coherence of an economy on whose regulators we wish, as far as possible, to throw light. But how to tackle such a complex subject? Two types of approach have been selected. The following chapter will be devoted to the sphere of production and the problem of growth. It seemed necessary to precede it by a chapter devoted to the sphere of exchange and the question of the relations between town and country. This choice, which may appear paradoxical, is justified for three reasons. Firstly, exchange or, more precisely, relations between town and village, take us to the heart of the system and thus provide a privileged observatory for its study. Secondly, it is in this domain that there appeared, during the course of the second half of the tenth century, the most important phenomenon of an economic order, an integral component of the feudal revolution, on a par with the end of slavery or the establishment of the territorial power of the castellans: the transformation of the town/country relationship and its corollary, the birth of the market. Thirdly, at a purely historiographical level, it is also the principal stumbling-block on which various currents of thought have come to grief. It would not, indeed, be without value to consider, as we progress, the reasons for such a general failure.

One problem and three failures

The enigma of urban fortunes

Let us start with a statement of the problem. The major questions in history are in practice always simple, and only the difficulty of answering them leads to a sort of false 'sophistication' in which the essence is lost from view. Since it is the economic history called 'medieval' which is at issue here, there exist not a thousand and one questions, but two, and only two. The rest is subsidiary. The first (which we will leave aside for the moment) concerns the take-off of the western economy, which was to give Europe a considerable technological advance over the rest of the world well before the emergence of capitalism. The other (our subject here) is the strange fate of the urban phenomenon. The point of departure is well known, that is the Roman civilisation of which the town was the keystone. The subsequent progress is quite clear, at least in its chronology. Up to the late tenth century, the town constantly lost ground, as if afflicted by dwarfism; by the end of the process, it was almost a phantom-town at the centre of a society which had been 'ruralised', to use the current and perfectly justified expression. The phenomenon is so striking that feudalism and ruralism are spontaneously associated by a process which is, to say the least, imprudent (it confuses chronology and logic). But it matters little; in the short run, the key fact is this massive, plurisecular, irrefutable trend. Then, suddenly, the trend was reversed, even more lastingly. Throughout the countryside, the urban buds multiplied and blossomed, a ranked network of towns (small, medium and large) was established. Interrupted by the crisis of the end of the 'Middle Ages' (by which is understood the crisis of feudalism), the movement resumed its course in the modern period. It is hardly necessary to emphasise the multiple implications of this double phenomenon; it shaped the medieval and the modern worlds.

The root problem, still unresolved, concerns the reversal of the trend round about the year 1000. In the immense literature devoted to the medieval town, everything but an answer to this problem is to be found. 'Everything' includes the description of the two processes in all their aspects: topographic, demographic, institutional, social . . . not to speak of such fashionable contemporary refinements as 'sociability' (urban and rural) and the perception of space (urban and rural).

To be fair, the reader will find an answer along the following lines: the town declined during the course of the 'High Middle Ages' because commercial activity contracted; it subsequently developed as a result of the revival of trade, even of a 'commercial revolution'. This splendid tautology does not much advance our understanding.

It has however the merit of directing the spotlight on to trade, where the key to the enigma may, in practice, lie concealed. But what difficulties this subject has caused! It would be possible to grasp the nettle, research its ups and downs, observe how it was articulated with production, or the social division of labour and so on. The question could even be posed (why not?) as to whether trade formed the same type of relations with the other economic categories before and after the year 1000, that is whether it occupied the same structural (or systematic) place. This might well lead on to fertile hypotheses about the trends in urban history. The smallest step in this direction however leads on to dangerous ground, that is the economic system, a taboo concept, since too impregnated with historical materialism. There is an instinctive tendency to extricate oneself from the difficulty by one or other of the two methods to hand: by considering the problem as resolved and falling back on the descriptive aspects referred to above, or by trying to explain the dynamic of trade without reference to the system, that is explaining trade . . . by trade, for example explaining the commercial revival of Europe by external mercantile influences. All the problematics of the last fifty years are the consequence of this intellectual cul-de-sac, as a brief survey will suffice to show.

Why the failure to progress?

The traditional (or positivist) approach is the one which pays least attention, obviously, to this problem. It is not without significance that French medievalists have long been divided into two categories: specialists in towns and specialists in the countryside. This has meant that the relationship between the two entities is rarely treated as a subject in its own right. It is tackled partially or accidentally, starting from those aspects which are directly illumined by the sources (population trends, reciprocal influences of institutions etc.). The question of the turn-round in urban history has not produced a specific problematic. The decline of the town has been seen as no more than one particular aspect of a more general decline; its subsequent revival as one particular aspect of a global growth, the town developing thanks to the appearance of an agricultural surplus, not forgetting, of course, demography . . . There is some truth in these views, but they are inadequate, especially in the light of the fact that the first period – as we now know – saw no decline in rural life.

The second approach is that of the 'exchangists', who put at the forefront of their analysis the phenomena of circulation. They include historians of considerable stature, reacting to the mediocrity of contemporary answers. Their finest representative was the Belgian historian Henri Pirenne, whose thesis caused something of a storm.[1] His schema is well known: the ruralisation of the West was the result of the irruption of Islam into the Mediterranean, which cut the axis of the ancient long-distance trade and consequently provoked the decline of trade and that of towns. Conversely, the re-opening of the Mediterranean by the crusaders and the reactivation of the North Sea by the Scandinavians created the conditions for a commercial and urban revival. After Pirenne, Maurice Lombard stood this thesis on its head and rehabilitated the role of Islam: in reviving to its own advantage long-distance Mediterranean trade and injecting gold into the West, it stimulated the commercial Renaissance.[2] Symmetrical conclusions, but identical premises, that is the same priority to the exogenous factor and the explanation of trade by trade. These two theories have suffered so many attacks that not much today survives. But even if their answers are far from satisfactory, we should recognise their merit in not having evaded the problem.

The third failure is that of the Marxist approach, a priori better equipped to tackle this type of problem, but which has manifestly been unable to integrate the question of towns into the feudal system. For this, there are, of course, general causes arising from the history of Marxism itself, which there is no need to spell out here. Let us look rather at the particular problems as they emerge in, for example, the work of one of the best Marxist historians, Maurice Dobb, in both his

Studies in the Development of Capitalism[3] and his famous debate with Paul Sweezy (an exchangist).[4]

We observe first a block with regard to the sphere of exchange, to the extent that it has been opposed to the sphere of production and consequently to the relations of production. The Dobb-Sweezy dialogue (à propos the transition from feudalism to capitalism) is illuminating in this regard. Sweezy:

We see thus how long-distance trade could be a creative force, bringing into existence a *system* of production for exchange alongside the old feudal system of production for use.[5]

Dobb:

There are even hints that these relations of exchange (by contrast with relations of production) are the focus of attention in Sweezy's interpretation of the historical process. (He regards 'the crucial feature of feudalism', for example, as being 'that it is a system of *production for use*'.) If this is so, then I think we have a fundamental issue between us. The definition which I was using in my *Studies* was advisedly in terms of the relations . . . between the direct producer and his overlord.[6]

Exchange on one side, production on the other; Dobb justifiably objected to a sort of conjuring away of what he considered to be the prime basis of every society, at the risk of no longer paying the attention it deserved to exchange. This was a tendency subsequently accentuated by Marxist historians.[7]

We cannot however reduce the problem to this insubstantial block. A profound theoretical notion predetermines it, one which will be discussed more fully at the end of this book. In a word, it is a matter of the common conception of the 'mode of production' reduced to 'relations of production', corresponding to a state of 'productive forces'. The idea is not so much wrong, in the last analysis, as incomplete, and to that extent, dangerous. It ignores the presence, visible though they are, of true socio-economic systems corresponding to the principal relations of exploitation, systems endowed with specific mechanisms and particular laws of functioning. This approach, whose finest exponents are Moses Finley[8] and Witold Kula,[9] has had only a marginal impact on those historians who invoke Marxism. We need look no further for explanations of the inability to resolve the problem posed. It is impossible to integrate one element (exchange) into a whole if, at the same time, one neglects the whole as a subject.

By means of this survey, we have tried to identify a problem (the turn-round of urban history), understand the reasons for such a protracted failure to make progress and, lastly, suggest a way forward: to study the place of exchange not horizontally (the geography of trade) but vertically (within the economic structure). We will discover whether the method adopted from the beginning of this study (micro-analysis in the service of a problematic based on the notion of system) is effective, and if it brings us closer, or not, to the solution. Let us return, then, to the Mâconnais, and focus our attention on the examination of town/country relations and their eventual transformation.

Mâcon and Lournand: a relationship of the ancient type

Distance: a major obstacle

In the first half of the tenth century, before Cluny had begun to develop an urban character, to a villager of Lournand the town meant Mâcon. Tournus, the other old town of the Mâconnais, in the shadow of the monastery of Saint-Philibert, site of a mint and a fair, was too far away to exercise much influence. Distance is, in effect, the prime consideration in an examination of town/country relations. The thirty kilometres separating Lournand and Mâcon, which included, further-more, a substantial range of hills, was then an insurmountable obstacle to the establishment of close and regular relations between them. For a man on horseback, certainly, the distance was short; but think of the peasant, especially if he had to drive a cartload of grain or wine drawn by a team of oxen. Historians of antiquity claim to have shown that it cost less to ship a cargo of grain from one end of the Mediterranean to the other than to cart it a distance of 120 kilometres.[10] Even if this is a slight exaggeration, the calculation has the virtue of drawing attention to the severity of the problems posed by the transport of merchandise. Not enough attention has perhaps been paid, in this connection, to the *revolution* which, on the plane of trade, was represented by the network of small towns or market towns which was established more or less everywhere from the eleventh century on, and which became one of the chief characteristics of the future feudal society. No peasant would then be further than seven or

eight kilometres from the nearest market. He could travel there and
back on the same day to sell eggs, butter or poultry. But we are not yet
there; we are still in a structure which condemned the village to
remoteness from the town and thus to isolation, with the exception of
those which ringed the city.[11] It is hardly necessary to insist that this
structure was directly inherited from Roman antiquity. Naturally, it
does not imply a total absence of reciprocal relations; links existed,
even if they were tenuous. But trade essentially took place within two
quite distinct contexts, almost strangers one to the other, and in very
different conditions. It should come as no surprise to discover that
they obeyed neither the same logic nor the same dynamic.

The primacy of the political function

Let us start with the urban context. Mâcon was an ancient Roman
town of average importance.[12] It was the administrative (hence origi-
nally fiscal) centre of a strongly Romanised circumscription (*civitas*),
and an important stage on a double axis of circulation, by river (the
Saône–Rhône axis) and by road (the Via Agrippa). The scatter of
sumptuous residences, their walls decorated with frescos, which surrounded the city was the most obvious sign of its former prosperity.
But, like all Roman cities, it had suffered a process of decline and
contraction, probably under way before the invasions. Fields and
vineyards took over a part of the space enclosed within its walls. At the
beginning of the tenth century, it was no more than the juxtaposition
of a few nuclei reduced to their simplest form. The comital nucleus, or
castrum, perched on a spur, inhabited by servants and a few armed
men, was where the count periodically assembled the tribunal which
was the guarantee of the peace of the *pagus*. Below lay the ecclesiastical
bourg, also walled, comprising the cathedral of Saint-Vincent, the
house of the bishop and the cloister of the chapter. Lastly, there was a
small merchant quarter, the *bourg* of Chavanne, dominated by the
presence of a Jewish colony, 'a foreign body encysted in the Christian
milieu'.[13] To these should be added three religious establishments
situated outside the walls: the abbey of Saint-Pierre to the west, the
abbey of Saint-Laurent across the Saône, and that of Saint-Clément
further to the south. How big was this 'urban' population? It is
impossible to say with any precision, but the modesty of the site
inclines one to think that it can hardly have exceeded 1,000 to 1,500
souls, including the agriculturalists living on curtilages within the

walls. The relative paucity of the urban population will stand out even more when we examine the demography of the countryside.

But we should look first at the way in which the various functions of the town interrelated. In the Roman period, the dominant function of a city was of a political order. It lived primarily from the revenues draining into it from its surroundings by the agency of the land tax, a part of which remained in the hands of its officers, its soldiers and, generally, of its elite, keystone of the social edifice. The economic functions were strictly subordinate to this basic political and social fact. The town, in effect, produced little or nothing for the benefit of the surrounding countryside. The crafts catered primarily to the needs of the privileged urban clientèle; the same was true of commercial activities, characterised by the diffusion throughout the towns of the Empire of a range of luxury products (precious cloths, perfumes, spices etc.), many of which came from the East. In other words, these economic activities took place within an almost hermetically sealed urban circuit, to which they did not bring revenue. They did not create the wealth of the town; they were, on the contrary, dependent on it, since they were dependent on the revenues of their urban clientèle, that is, in the last analysis on the capacity of the town to exploit the rural world surrounding it. This is a specific and significant aspect of a dependence of the economic on the political, from which we should conclude that urban development was primarily the expression of the development of the state itself or of its fiscal capacity.

Had this specifically ancient type of articulation been modified? In form, yes, but not in its nature. The ancient bureaucracy had certainly disappeared, only to be replaced by an administrative embryo – or rather, residue – around the count, but the religious function had taken over from the political function, in the strict sense. Mâcon had become the town of the bishop, the clerk replacing the functionary. This transfer from the political to the religious should not however conceal the essence, that is the primacy of the extra-economic function (power in another form) in the tenth-century town, a primacy at least as strong as, if not stronger than, in the past. The economic functions of Mâcon continued to be ordered according to the same model. The products of its few artisans could not be destined for the peasants of the county, who were in no position to pay for them, given that the town was too remote to visit in order to sell their produce. Alone among the inhabitants of the countryside, the little group of masters, periodically drawn to Mâcon by their military or judicial obligations, constituted an occasional clientèle. They perhaps from time to time procured ornaments or arms in the town, though the iron working of the High Middle Ages tended to be dispersed in rural forges which were closer to the minerals and fuel. At least, the masters disposed of products which could be turned into cash, and which they were in a better position than the rest to despatch to Mâcon: the products of stock farming, especially the numerous pigs fattened in the woods of the Grosne valley. But the basic clientèle was the urban clientèle properly speaking: the count, his followers, the *familia* or entourage of the bishop, and those of the chapter and the abbeys. The artisans, many of whom were probably their former servants, catered for their needs. And if Mâcon remained a stage on one of the principal routes of a long distance commerce, in practice pretty desultory, it was because this clientèle continued to demand the luxury products of which the Jewish merchants remained the privileged intermediaries, thanks to the networks which they alone had been able to maintain. The commercial function thus remained highly dependent on the purchasing power of the urban clientèle, that is on the political function (in the wide sense of the word) of the town.

Did there at the very least exist a local commercial function based on supplying the city with provisions? The answer is, once again, mediated by the primacy of the 'political'. Requirements in grain and wine were for the most part met by the ecclesiastical and comital estates, the *servitium* of their slaves and the rents of their *coloni*. Their landed possessions were, in fact, highly concentrated around Mâcon, within a radius of less than seven or eight kilometres, the only way of surmounting the problem of transport. Salt, a product then indispensable in the preservation of foodstuffs, came from the comital saltpans of the nearby Revermont. The products of tithe, lastly, or at least whatever reached Mâcon after the local distributions to the clergy who saw to their collection, also contributed to the provisioning of the town. The evidence suggests that most of what the town consumed came from a circuit which was non-commercial. This is not to deny the existence of a traffic in foodstuffs. André Deléage pointed to the existence of a series of *portus* between Mâcon and Belleville,[14] which he linked to the structures of long distance trade, but which Georges Duby preferred to see as locales for peasant transactions.[15] The two hypotheses are not mutually exclusive, and it is highly probable that the presence of such a convenient means of water transport encouraged a flow of merchandise towards Mâcon. But the principal fact remains the primacy of the tributary relationship in the provisioning of Mâcon. The mercantile sphere was confined to a secondary, not to say marginal, role, subordinate, at all events, to the preceding circuit.

We may therefore draw three conclusions with regard to the urban economy. Firstly, at the local level, the market economy was necessarily embryonic, confined to the interstices of the 'tributary' circuit. Secondly, the market phenomena could only develop within long distance trade, on the basis of scarce products circulating within a vast geographical area which may be described as 'international'. Lastly, the primary economic activity of Mâcon (or of any other city of this type), that is the redistribution of the products of long distance trade, was 'imprisoned' within its political function, regulated by the degree of ascendancy which the town was in a position to exercise over the territory subject to its domination. Once this simple observation is accepted, it becomes fruitless to engage in interminable speculation as to the role of geopolitical factors in the evolution of long distance trade, as the 'exchangist' historians have done, even if, on occasion, these factors played some role. The dominant factor was internal; it lay in the decline of urban domination over the countryside, a decline of which the disappearance of the land tax was one of the most striking signs, but not the only one. In a word, it lay in the weakness of the state.

By the same token, we should resolutely eschew the notion that urban decline was a reflection of rural decline. The study of their functions shows rather that there was, in a sense, a disconnection between the urban and rural economies. The prosperity of the countryside could perfectly well coexist with the decline of the town if the latter was no longer in a position to maintain the level of its levies. Logic would even suggest that a reduction of urban parasitism would be a factor for agrarian growth, and that this, in return, by modifying the equilibrium between town and country, would reduce the capacity of the former to structure and exploit the latter – a cumulative process, in fact.

One final comment cannot be avoided: the place of the tenth-century town in the economic structure was of the same nature as in the 'ancient system'. Simply, we see it here in the final stage of the decomposition of the system, going down with the shipwrecked state.

The town remained exclusively parasitical. It is in striking contrast with the 'medieval' (or rather 'feudal') town, the economy of which was closely articulated with the rural economy. In these circumstances, nothing is more misleading than to speak of the 'town' in general, without any qualifier, except to indicate a simple concentration of individuals in a restricted physical space. The 'ancient town', or town enclosed in the ancient system, was characterised by a precise and specific hierarchy of functions, from which derived the logic of its growth or its decline. In this sense, Mâcon remained an ancient town.

The isolation of the countryside

Let us now return to Lournand and consider the role played there by trade. With regard, firstly, to trade between country and town, the situation is hardly in doubt; the village suffered a sort of isolation which condemned it to self-sufficiency. From the town, as we have seen, it received little or nothing. Tools and the objects in everyday use (clothes, pottery etc.) were products of local manufacture. This was usually within a domestic setting, the peasant family supplying its own needs. Other objects were produced by rural artisans. Unfortunately, the texts are so concerned to emphasise juridical condition that they leave in obscurity any specialisations of an economic type which might have existed. The reference to a couple of shoemakers at Varanges is exceptional;[16] 'peasant-shoemakers', we ought to say, since they lived on a curtilage surrounded by a vineyard and fields. There was as yet no division of labour separating the artisanate from agricultural activity, and it is reasonable to think that many small allod-holders were of necessity in a similar condition. More obscure still is the participation of slaves in this craft function. Since antiquity there had existed a direct link between the servile condition and the practice of 'mechanical' trades regarded as degrading and, all in all, less honourable than work on the land. Who else but the slaves built the mills in the Grosne valley and operated them on behalf of their masters? Their exclusion from ownership pushed them in the direction of the crafts just as the social exclusion of the Jews impelled them towards trade. Thanks to the institution of the *peculium*, which left them the profits of their labour, they could win a minimum of economic autonomy.

It seems, therefore, as if, below the urban economy, there was a vast subterranean (or 'infra-economic') economy, overwhelmingly agrarian, certainly, but endowed with considerable autonomy thanks to a far from negligible artisanal component. Were these two circuits separated by a watertight partition? No, there were passageways linking one to the other. The economy of the masters implied an outlet to the town, and formed a tenuous point of contact. The clergy spent money locally – as can be seen from their acquisitions of land – some of which might come from the town. A thin trickle of coins thus penetrated the countryside which could not, in any case, have lived in total self-sufficiency, since certain indispensable products, notably salt, were lacking.

Links therefore existed, but the salient fact remains the profound gulf separating the urban from the rural economy. It follows that trade was essentially intra-rural.

Barter in all its forms

What form did trade take? In the first place, that of barter. We have seen in the preceding chapter that land transactions in the first half of the century were overwhelmingly dominated by the practice of the exchange of parcels. If this was the case with the circulation of land, there is all the more reason to think that barter must have predominated in the circulation of ordinary goods, especially when we consider the inconvenience – not to speak of the scarcity – of the monetary tool, lacking coinage of low value. In addition to exchanges of land for land, barter took many forms. One was the exchange of labour for foodstuffs. This was the only way that a small allod-holder, incapable of meeting the needs of his household from his inadequate holding, could procure additional grain; he could enter the service of a better endowed neighbour, even a master, in return for some food (we will avoid the use of the word 'wage', which risks giving the erroneous impression of a labour market). Another form of barter was the exchange of labour for land. We have already had occasion to mention the frequent use of the contract of *méplant*, by which an owner entrusted the breaking up and initial cultivation of a piece of land to a peasant to whom, several years later, he granted half of the land which had been assarted. This was surely in practice a form of barter.

Another form was the exchange of goods for goods. This was probably a method of circulation of the products of craftsmen as much as of agricultural produce strictly speaking. The vine, for example, present everywhere, even on the tiniest holdings, provided a product particularly suitable to being exchanged for grain. Lastly, credit itself, based on the practice of the mortgage (which left the creditor the revenues of a pledged piece of land) may be analysed in terms of barter.

Thus exchange, as an economic act, was deeply embedded in social relations, determined more by relations of force than by the law of the market; no true labour market, no true grain market and, in consequence, no real land market either, as has been shown. In other words, no market, in the sense of the coming together of an offer and a demand endowed with a minimum of autonomy. This central phenomenon, without which the future feudal revolution becomes, to my mind, unintelligible, should be compared with the analysis made by Moses Finley for the Late Empire; with this difference only, that the state no longer in the tenth century played such a direct or constricting role as it had previously played to paralyse the mechanisms of the market. Nevertheless, the political and social structure, by maintaining the town/country gulf, and by allowing only a trickle of money to reach the village, still sufficed to maintain, in this regard, a situation of the ancient type.

Did there at least exist markets, in other words, a mercantile sector, alongside barter? Georges Duby thought that there did, claiming that markets were held every week near even the most isolated churches.[17] He is probably right, even if the references at our disposal are in general rather later. We know, in any case, that the countryside had experienced a sudden commercial flurry at the beginning of the Carolingian period. Manifestly, barter was no longer adequate to respond to the needs of local trade. In the long term, many factors promoted the latter's growth. The increasing autonomy of small family production – that major fact of the High Middle Ages – had as a natural consequence the search for autonomy in trade. The diminution of the power of masters over their slaves opened up a larger economic space to slave initiative. The first intimations of the social decline of the small allod-holders had the effect of stimulating their artisanal and mercantile activities. And behind all these phenomena there lurked another, of a more general character, which we have not yet had opportunity to mention: agrarian growth, in its double dimension, both qualitative and quantitative. It inevitably promoted a revival of trade, exercising its full effect on those micromarkets still confined in rural space, but ready to break out.

The decline of long distance trade and the emergence of a local market were two contradictory phenomena in two distinct spheres; there were also two different logics: on the one hand, the effect of the loosening of the political corset which confined society from the top; on the other, the slow pressure from below of economic forces which one can faintly discern though not yet see clearly. Was there a connection between these two logics? It is too soon to say. Let us look first at how the arrival of the monks modified the situation in the vicinity of Cluny.

Cluny and Lournand: a relationship of a new type

By the beginning of the eleventh century, the structures of exchange were radically different, the old town/country relations disrupted and the picture we have drawn no longer applicable. We will examine this development in the narrow context of the Cluny region to remain within the perspective of a micro-history, but we should bear in mind that we are not discussing a unique event, attributable to the chance wanderings of Berno and his companions. The transformation was general; it affected, with some chronological variations here and there, the entire West; it modified the course of its development, suddenly reversing the graph of urban life, which it now sent in an upwards direction.

How should we characterise this change? Its most immmediate and most visible aspect was the establishment of a close relationship between town and country, that is a total reversal of the previous situation, where the separation between the two was maximal. Town and country were linked one to the other to the point where their respective development became for a long time interdependent. But there is more to it than this highly visible dimension. More profound was the change which gave trade a new, and increasingly important, place at the centre of the economy. It is from this period that the market (in its general sense) tended to become a mechanism which regulated the economy, and we witness the emergence of an 'economy' endowed for the first time with its own dynamic; consequently, in a sense, the birth of the economy, finally freed from the political corset within which it had been confined. This is something we should remember, incidentally, as the 'socialist' countries propose to implement a restoration of the market: the market is in no way a category of capitalism. Feudalism had already given it a powerful impetus, though assigning to it certain limits which it was able to maintain for several centuries. To associate feudalism with self-sufficiency or isolation is surely the gravest error it is possible to commit in its regard. It inhibited trade, certainly, on the eve of its existence, when it maintained frontiers which had become too narrow given the new pressure of economic forces. In due course, however, it liberated these forces, hitherto enclosed in the little cells of the rural world. It did so by the creation of a new context which allowed a new social division of labour and the establishment of a new relationship, dominated by trade, between town and country.

The new contexts for trade

Let us first define the context, before discussing the consequences of its establishment. It consisted, firstly, of a strictly delineated territory, subject to a local power which may now be described as seigneurial. In the most common case, it was the 'district' placed under the authority of a castellan. In our particular case, it was the territory placed under the 'sacred *ban*' of the monastery by the end of the political process described above, that is a progression from a *de facto* immunity to a legal immunity. By 955 the outcome was assured; the process was completed during the following decades by the establishment of monastic jurisdiction, the elimination of comital influence and the subjection of the most turbulent warriors. It was a restricted territory since the circle within which the abbey's *ban* was exercised never exceeded seven kilometres in radius; beyond, and not without friction over the boundaries, the power of the neighbouring castellans (Berzé, Uxelles etc.) was being established in parallel.

Secondly, on the economic plane, this territory was organised around a town/country duo. By the second half of the century, Cluny had in effect assumed an urban character. Naturally, the exceptional growth of the monastery gave it a peculiarly clerical atmosphere. Among the new inhabitants of the agglomeration, many had an activity connected with the presence of the monks (servants, certain artisans etc.). This did not prevent the development outside the monastic enclosure of a *bourg* – round the parish church of Saint-Maïeul – the inhabitants of which, carefully distinguished from the country dwellers of the environs, were called 'burgesses' before the year 1000.[18]

By then, for the villagers in its vicinity, the town which concerned them was no longer Mâcon but Cluny. It was a town which, for the first time in history, was within easy reach, and they could frequent its weekly market, meeting-point for the products of an urban artisanate increasingly geared to rural needs and the produce of the land. This was the crucial factor, absent from the ancient structure: the establishment of a commercial relationship between town and country, of a bilateral relationship, no longer exclusively tributary. The tributary relationship did not, of course, disappear. The monastic barns and cellars received the tithes and rents of the peasantry. But alongside had been born a commercial relationship between two partners whose respective activities were linked in a common dialectic of development: the local town was an outlet for the agricultural surplus; the surrounding countryside was a market gradually opening up to the urban craftsmen. We see a logic of development which stimulated both agrarian growth and the expansion of the secondary and tertiary functions of the town; a basically economic logic, consequently, which broke with the previous containment of the economic function of the town within its political function.

Lastly, the district was equipped with a series of institutions which were favourable to trade: the weekly market, with, in the middle of the following century, periodic fairs. Most important of all, the abbey had by 930 received the right to mint money. It is difficult to appreciate the actual effects of this, as the texts do not specify the origin of the coins in circulation. However, we have seen that the earlier separation of the two economic circuits (urban and rural) had allowed only a thin trickle of money to penetrate the countryside and therefore condemned it to the widespread practice of barter. The situation was now transformed. Not only could the monastery inject more cash, but the monetary circuit, now shorter than that which had gravitated around Mâcon, allowed a more rapid circulation of coins.

This was not the result, obviously, of a conscious economic rationality, but of primarily fiscal intentions: the monks thereby channelled the forces of trade and drew from them generous profits. Nor did it alone determine the growth of trade. It would not have been effective if it had not responded to profound needs, notably resulting from agrarian growth and hitherto contained by the persistence of ancient structures. Other factors, furthermore, contributed to the penetration of money into the region. As Georges Duby observed, the prestige of the abbey attracted a growing number of merchants and pilgrims, who had money to spend. But we should not succumb to the temptation to resort yet again to an exogenous interpretation by explaining – at the risk of locking into a circular argument – the commercial revival of the district round Cluny by a more favourable environment. At the end of the day, it is the revival of trade throughout the West which we need to understand. And in this regard, no factor was more general than the sudden transformation (even if its chronology varied from one region to another) of the relationship between town and country, with the establishment of a close connection between these two elements within restricted territorial units.

Pandora's box

The proof, it seems to me, lies in the speed with which the economic atmosphere changed at the precise period when this structure was put into place. We have already noted the sudden explosion of the land market from the 970s: a rapid substitution of sale for the barter of parcels and a five- or six-fold increase in the price of land in less than thirty years. This must surely imply an equally sudden increase in the means of payment and the speed of its circulation. And if a market was thus established in land, it is hard to believe that it did not also extend to common products, especially agricultural. The frequency of famines recorded around the year 1000 may well also be connected with this phenomenon.[19] We are emerging from a socio-economic system (the 'ancient system') in which market forces were imprisoned by a whole complex of political and social structures. It is as if, in a last convulsion of its long agony, it opened a Pandora's box by its liberation of these forces. This constitutes an obscure, but not the least important, aspect of the 'feudal revolution': the social transformation which had long been on the horizon had come up against the extra-ordinary stability of the free peasantry, which retained control over its land precisely because this control was shielded from the pernicious influence of money and the market. The irruption of money called everything into question. The only sure way for a peasant to hold on to the land he tilled was to concede ownership of it to the church, so he could retain its usufruct. The explosion of the market thus paved the way for the generalisation of tenure and, reciprocally, the system of tenure made it possible to cool the stakes with regard to land by controlling the destructive effects of the market. This last point illustrates a central feature of feudalism; it was a social system which, while deriving strength from the development of the market, kept the market within certain limits by a whole institutional, social and ideological apparatus.

It remains the case that the market was born or, more precisely, that it emerged from the very narrow sphere within which it had been contained. It henceforward played a major role in the remodelling of European society. One illustration of this is to be found in the new relationship established between town and country: it shows clearly the extent of the changes which had been experienced during the processes of the transformation of society, one sign among many of the transition from one system to another.

Interdependence and inequality

We have observed a sort of disconnection between the urban and the rural dynamics during the High Middle Ages or the period of the destructuring of ancient society. This was even expressed by an inversion in their development: the decline of the town of the ancient type on the basis of agrarian growth. But the respective development of the town and the countryside from the eleventh century on is posed in new terms, which can be summed up in two words: inter-dependence and inequality.

There was interdependence in the sense that the growth of one fostered the growth of the other. Urban growth was now based on a gradual penetration of rural space, that is on the enlargement of its surrounding market. It benefited both from gross agricultural growth and from the degree to which the peasant economy was penetrated by the market, hence the rate of commercialisation of agricultural pro-duction. The small and market towns whose roots were wholly rural were naturally its first beneficiaries. But it was, in the end, the whole of the urban network – including its hierarchy of medium-sized and large towns, their functions increasingly diversified – which, by a sort of capillary action, was nourished by agricultural growth.

Conversely, rural growth was stimulated by the urban presence. The peasant economy was no longer turned in on itself according to the Chayanov model. The prospect of buying consumer goods in an urban market was for the peasant an incitement to produce more and sell his surplus. We should not yet see this as the profit motive, but simply the desire to procure certain goods. In any case, the peasantry was very early concerned to improve its conditions of access to the urban market by the elimination of seigneurial monopolies and the reduction of the fiscal burden weighing on trade. This can clearly be seen in the place occupied by such issues in the charters of franchise extracted from the seigneurial class. The peasant of the feudal age was first defined in terms of relations of production: he was a small producer, possessor of a tenure and subject to seigneurial dues. However, it should not be forgotten that he was also linked, in a new and original way, to the market and that his economic behaviour was thereby profoundly influenced: this was a major consequence of the transformation of the relations between town and country.[20] Thus, the two elements of the town/country duo were interdependent in growth. This is not, of course, to attribute the spectacular economic expansion of the eleventh to thirteenth centuries solely to the intervention of this single factor. But that this interdependence was new, and that it was a powerful stimulus, cannot be denied.

However, the interdependence of their respective development was marked by an inequality in favour of the town. This is a large and much neglected problem, which would repay considerable research in view of its numerous implications. Its effects are more clearly perceived than its causes. These were probably of two types. The first, socio-economic, were the consequence of the asymmetry in trade between the peasant and the townsman. The former was manifestly in a position of inferiority, since he was above all a producer and consumer of 'use values' – to employ a Marxist formulation – the market value of which he appreciated only with difficulty, whereas it was market value which primarily interested the townsman. The other cause of the inequality was probably of a more general, almost political, character. Fernand Braudel has provided an excellent description of the subordinate relation between country and town:

The *bourg* essentially stood for domination: it reigned over a rural district . . . (it) not only represented social and economic superiority: it was also the seat of the first tier of law and order. Similarly, above the *bourgs*, there was the town, which stood above all for domination, and which laid down its circles of influence (demographic, provisioning, commercial).[21]

This disequilibrium probably explains the uneven development of the town and the countryside within the feudal system: urban growth was manifestly stronger. The speed of the process of urbanisation from the eleventh century on provides proof. We should not be surprised. The superiority the town enjoyed enabled it to appropriate numerous revenues and made it a place where wealth was concentrated. And money in its turn attracted men. A constant and generalised migratory flow was established from the country to the town: it was one of the major characteristics of the new demographic structures, inseparable from the social system itself. This represented another break with the previous situation, when the rural population lacked any urban outlet, the town of the ancient type being too rigid an organism for the absorption of such an influx to be conceivable. We appreciate here, let it be said in passing, the artificial or arbitrary character of any global approach by a so-called 'medieval demography' which does not first take into account this fundamental structural change.

The town progressed, therefore, at a more rapid pace than the country in terms of revenues, population and even productivity of labour (in favour of an increasingly developed division of labour). It dragged, in a sense, the agricultural sector behind it as far as this was possible, demanding from it food and raw materials, and giving it new orientations, which were sometimes of a speculative type. It was a dynamising factor, but, in the end, exhausting. The inequality of development introduced into the socio-economic system was an insurmountable contradiction: sooner or later the town outgrew the space which provisioned it. The breaking point was obviously reached when the possibilities of agricultural expansion in space were exhausted, that is during the thirteenth century. We touch here on one aspect of the crisis of the system evident around 1300.

Another system

But let us not anticipate. These few remarks made in passing are intended only to emphasise the existence, after the year 1000, of trends which profoundly affected the development or transformation of the economy and of society. They bear no relationship to the earlier trends of the fifth to tenth centuries. Or, in other words, society and the economy functioned in a radically different way. And it is clear that these new trends and the logic which articulated them were linked to the major innovation whose importance cannot be exaggerated: the emergence of a market permeating the whole of western society. We must be clear what this means. The rupture of the year 1000 was far more profound than is generally appreciated. It affected society from top to bottom. It expressed the transition from one social system to another: the death knell of ancient society, the baptism of feudal society.

The unequivocal nature of this assertion may cause surprise. It is entirely in line, however, with a revision begun by others some decades ago; it does no more than push the logic a little further. To pursue this point for a moment: the time is not long gone when historians of the 'Middle Ages' defined feudal society by vassalage and the fief, as if a criterion relating to hardly more than 3 or 4 per cent of the population could be employed to characterise a society in its entirety. They were succumbing to an old reflex which consisted of having eyes only for the dominant class. It was a great step forward when certain historians (Robert Boutruche and Jacques Le Goff among others) emphasised the connection between fief and seigneurie. Under the influence, direct or indirect, of Marxism, attention was no longer focused only on the 'roof' of the social edifice but on its structure as a whole; the relations between the rulers and the ruled could thus find a place. But there remained the obstacle presented by the vexed question of the genesis of the structure, which a deeply-entrenched tradition associated more or less explicitly with the fall of the Roman Empire and the Germanic invasions, from which derived the personal ties which prefigured vassalage. This led to the elaboration of incautious schemas as to 'feudal ages' (the first Carolingian age, the second feudal age etc.) which confused, more than they clarified, the issue.

The next step was decisive and largely prepared the ground for the revisions now under way. It is attributable to Georges Duby, also evidently influenced by Marxism, notably in his vision of the state and ideology. The first to appreciate that the rupture of the year 1000 was decisive, he analysed it in its double dimension, both political (the appearance of a new apparatus of power) and ideological (the appearance of a new dominant ideology).[22] The expression 'feudal revolution', aureoled by his magisterial authority, thus entered historical discourse. But Georges Duby hesitated on the question of social change and did not continue down the path he had himself opened up. This could be because he went on to concentrate on questions of *mentalités*, or he may have been impeded by his vision of servitude. Duby saw the *servi* of the tenth century as medieval serfs and thus believed that the essential social change had taken place before the feudal revolution, which was a sort of political conclusion to the process. But beyond this divergence of analysis of a formal nature lies a basic agreement, whose epistemological roots are clear: the search for a necessary fertilisation of historical materialism by the principles aquired from the human sciences.

However that may be, Pierre Bonnassie took the baton from Georges Duby and made another step forward by emphasising the persistence of slavery into the tenth century. Since the publication of his article, his views have not seriously been challenged, and the transformation of the tenth century has assumed, thanks to him, a new social dimension and density. The train transporting us towards a new reading of the transition from ancient to feudal society was under way. The present chapter tries to attach an extra coach, by asserting that to the changes already observed we need to add those affecting economic structures and, in so doing, consider the significance of the whole congeries of changes. They surely bear a strong resemblance to a revolution in the full sense of the term.

From our examination of trade, let us note, in conclusion, these two closely connected phenomena: the sudden emergence of the market and the transformation of town/country relations. We see here only, let us be clear, the sign or indicator of the transition to another socio-economic system, quite different from what preceded it. The system was not defined by the place held in it by the mechanism of exchange; it was above all a new configuration of the classes or, if preferred, it was based on a 'relation of production' for which the seigneurie became the primary context – on this there can be no ambiguity. But we should observe that the establishment of new social relations was accompanied by new economic structures and that the place occupied by trade was one of their characteristics. Those who, within a comparative perspective, ponder the possible existence of a feudalism outside Europe (one thinks here of India, China and Japan) would be well advised to study not only social relations but also, as an indicator, the development of town/country relations.

Lastly, let us keep in mind the principal problem, that is the sudden appearance of the market. It was a phenomenon strictly circumscribed in time since it can be dated to within a few years (around 970). The chronology makes plain the link with political developments. The establishment of seigneurial domination acted as a trigger or catalyst, by the organisation of an economic space endowed with the appropriate tools. But it might be supposed that the phenomenon responded to more profound causes of a social and economic order. The disintegration of power would not have had such an effect had there not been a soil favourable to the rapid growth of trade. Let us now look for these profound causes in an examination of agrarian growth.

Notes

1 H. Pirenne, *Mohammed and Charlemagne*, London, 1939.
2 Maurice Lombard, 'L'or musulman du VIe au XIe siècle', *Annales-ESC*, 1947.
3 Maurice Dobb, *Studies in the Development of Capitalism*, Cambridge, 1946.
4 Maurice Dobb and Paul Sweezy, *The Transition from Feudalism to Capitalism*, Introduction by Rodney Hilton, London, 1976.
5 Sweezy, *The Transition*, p. 42.
6 Dobb, *The Transition*, p. 58.
7 Another illustration of this trend is the underestimation of the role played by the hypertrophy of the town in the crisis of the feudal system, in my *Crisis of Feudalism*:
8 Finley, *Ancient Economy*.
9 Witold Kula, *Théorie économique du système féodal*, Paris–The Hague, 1970 (translated by Lawrence Garner as *An Economic Theory of the Feudal System*, London, 1976).
10 A. H. M. Jones, *The Later Roman Empire*, Oxford, 1964, pp. 841–2.
11 Herein lies the exceptional nature of the suburban countryside, location par excellence of the classical estate system.
12 Emile Magnien, *Histoire de Mâcon et du Mâconnais*, Mâcon, 1971.
13 Duby, *La Société . . . dans la région mâconnaise*, p. 110.
14 Deléage, *Vie rurale en Bourgogne*, pp. 174–5.
15 Duby, *La Société . . . dans la région mâconnaise*, p. 50.
16 C. C. 670 (948).
17 Duby, *La Société . . . dans la région mâconnaise*, p. 49.
18 C. C. 2225.
19 Vivid testimony in Raoul Glaber, who expresses surprise at the astronomical prices of foodstuffs.
20 The adherents of an unchanging 'peasant mode of production', closed in on itself, indifferent to the society surrounding it, should reflect on this major rupture in 1000. For the earlier period, their analysis is not without foundation; after 1000, in contrast, the peasant tends to become an economic subject with all that this entails, his activity integrated into a larger whole.
21 Fernand Braudel, *l'Identité de la France*, vol. I, p. 142 (translated by Siân Reynolds as *The Identity of France*, London, 1988).
22 Duby, *The Three Orders*.

4

Agrarian growth

I turn now to the sphere of production. The delay in doing so may cause some surprise, since local monographs generally begin with a global discussion of the occupation of the soil together with, to the extent that this is possible, an examination of settlement. Logic might also prefer production to have preceded trade. However, the question of production is by far the most difficult to grasp, technically and intellectually. It therefore seemed preferable to clear the surrounding ground before tackling this most hazardous of obstacles.

The technical difficulties derive from the fact that the productive activities leave fewer traces in the sources than do transactions. The only aspect about which we are well informed is the distribution of the cultivated area between the various activities: around one fifth vines, one tenth meadow, a slightly smaller proportion in curtilages and manses (including gardens), the rest devoted to cereals, the basic element in traditional polyculture. We also have evidence, it is true, as to the main features of the way land was divided up, that is the morphology and dimensions of parcels, enclosures, access roads etc. But this aspect, interesting though it is, will be left aside (it has, in any case, been very thoroughly dealt with by André Deléage), since the structure of the holdings is only very indirectly relevant to the dynamic perspective which is our main concern. It is important for us to establish the trend of production rather than read an agrarian landscape whose main features were already fixed, the successive sedimentations of agrarian civilisations since the neolithic. The living tissue, if I may venture the expression, has been preferred to the dead, the active historical factor to the residual trace. Our problem is to discover what were the tools, the cultural techniques, the yields in grain, on the basis of the dry notices and charters recording the transmission of parcels from one hand to another.

The question is intellectually difficult because a process of growth in a traditional or pre-capitalist economy cannot be analysed in simpler terms than a contemporary economy. It needs both micro-analysis (notably of the behaviour of the economic agents) and macro-analysis (of the distribution and circulation of revenues, the relationship between population and resources etc.). To undertake its study on the basis of material so laconic may seem a foolhardy venture. The attempt, nevertheless, must be made, while recognising in so doing the persistence of substantial grey areas. After all, these are, let us be in no doubt, crucial questions for the understanding of the historical process as a whole and for our very vision of feudal society. What was the origin of the basic impulsions to growth? When and how were they manifested?

The problematic: one certainty and two unknowns

A rapid rehearsal of the problematic is necessary before we turn the microscope once again on to the region of Cluny. It can be organised around one certainty (the evidence for 'medieval' growth) and two unknowns or uncertainties (its precise chronology and mainsprings).

The classical schema of medieval growth

'Medieval' growth, taken as a whole, is a key fact in the history of Europe. It was in the first place agrarian growth, manifesting two forms: qualitative (technical progress) and quantitative or extensive (an increase in the cultivated area). The latter is the better known. It was the result of dogged clearance of woodland and the conquest of marshy or easily flooded lands. It did not end until some point during the course of the thirteenth century (or at the latest the early fourteenth century in certain regions), by which time the assarters had access only to mediocre lands capable of providing only uncertain or declining yields; at the same time, the equilibrium between forest (a reservoir of foodstuffs for animals and men) and fields necessary to traditional agriculture had been broken by the excessive advance of the latter.

The immense task of conquering new lands was made easier by a group of technical improvements which, as Georges Duby has correctly observed, constituted the greatest leap forward since the neolithic.[1] Its principal element consisted of a greater mastery of various sources of energy. In the first place, water power was mastered thanks to the diffusion into the most remote villages of an effective piece of machinery (known since antiquity), the water-mill; this freed a large amount of working time previously absorbed by the operation of hand mills or pestles. Secondly, a greater mastery of animal power was achieved by the adoption of new techniques of harnessing (the horn yolk for oxen, the rigid shoulder collar for horses). The other improvements were closely connected to these two. The greater capacity of animal traction allowed the adoption of more efficient ploughing tools, either by the improvement of the old swing plough (*araire*) of Mediterranean origin or by the introduction of a wheeled plough (*charrue*); the *charrue* was able to turn the soil over, reactivating more effectively its fertilising elements and, above all, was suited to the heavy soils which the *araire* had found so difficult. Last but by no means least, the increases in the productivity of labour made possible an increase in the frequency with which the soil was dressed, in particular in the number of ploughings. One of the most fruitful innovations in this regard was the three-course rotation (winter corn, spring corn, fallow), which was substituted throughout a large part of Europe (with the exception of the southern regions) for the old two-course rotation which left the land resting one year in two.

To put this technological leap forward into perspective, we need only remember that European agriculture survived for many centuries on this basis, without significant change, that is using the same tools and the same agricultural techniques. Up to the end of the nineteenth century, only minor, though clearly not negligible, improvements were made, such as an increase in the use of iron in tools, the importation of plants from the New World, better sorting of seeds. It was only with chemical fertilisers and agricultural machinery that the traditional technical equilibrium was broken in favour of a true agricultural revolution.[2]

Chronology

It is more difficult to establish a reliable chronology of agrarian expansion, in particular whether it followed the establishment of feudal structures or whether it to some degree preceded them. This is the real question, which has enormous theoretical implications for the respective role of technical and social factors in a process of development. The traditional response favoured the central period of the 'Middle Ages', which was presented as the period of the greatest progress, and not without reason. Reference has been made to the intensity of assarting, especially in northern Europe, which culminated in the twelfth century; also to the appearance of numerous mills and the increasing use of iron in agricultural implements. These indicators are corroborated by a demographic progress which is difficult to measure, certainly, but which everything suggests was regular and which culminated, despite its slow pace, in an exceptional situation of overpopulation around 1300. From this to the conclusion that it was the new feudal structures which were crucial was but a small step. Thus a Marxist historian, Charles Parain, linked the diffusion of the water-mill directly to the seigneurial system; it was necessary, he said, for a lord to control the banks of the water-course before he would contemplate building a mill and, above all, for him to be in a position to benefit from seigneurial charges (*banalités*) before he would accept such an investment.[3] Georges Duby also favoured the twelfth and thirteenth centuries in his *Rural Economy and Country Life in the Medieval West*; soon after he gave a theoretical expression to this analysis by seeing the demands of seigneurial fiscality (and, in consequence, of the *seigneurie banale*) as the spur which goaded the peasantry to even greater production.[4]

This view no longer receives such universal acceptance. The unevenness of the sources available for the two periods under consideration distorts the historian's view; the fact that the more recent documentation is also the more abundant inclines historians to register only the obvious manifestations of progress in the eleventh to twelfth centuries and underestimate the earlier signs of development, concealed in a general semi-obscurity. However, most recent research relating to specific technical improvements (the mill, the wheeled plough, the use of the horse, new types of harness, the three-course rotation etc.) tends to put the medieval 'technological revolution' and, by the same token, the lift-off of agrarian growth, rather earlier (in the ninth and tenth centuries, sometimes even earlier), though accepting, of course, that it continued beyond, on the basis of the momentum it had acquired. This is a schema which needs some qualification according to region. In areas of precocious agrarian colonisation (Catalonia, the south of France), where, consequently, settlement was already far advanced by the Roman period, the possibilities for extending the cultivated area in space were obviously limited, so that the second phase of medieval growth was less spectacular in these regions. Conversely, the further one progresses towards northern Europe, where wooded wastes still covered large stretches of ground, the more important was this second phase.

The thesis of a precocious agrarian growth which was essentially Carolingian seems now therefore to be firmly on the agenda. The last Flaran Colloquium (September 1988), which assembled some of the finest European specialists in this field, only brought further confirmation. 'Alone against the world', to use his own expression, Robert Fossier maintained the traditional point of view with almost pathetic vigour; true, the revision under way calls into question themes dear to Fossier's heart: the 'birth of Europe' and the 'birth of the village' as phenomena which postdated the year 1000. To admit a precocious chronology of growth also involves a re-evaluation of the respective role of the technical and the social, which has to be conceived in more dialectical terms. The establishment of feudal structures can no longer be seen as the starting point for medieval growth, even if its role in the consolidation and expansion of this development is evident. What has earlier been said on the subject of the emergence of the market and the reversal of the town/country relationship is an early illustration of this. Conversely, the question of what influence technical progress and agrarian growth exercised on the social transformation itself is posed, and in new terms. History provides, after all, other examples of social destabilisation induced by a process of growth (one thinks, in particular, of eighteenth-century Europe).

The mainsprings

That said, there remains outstanding the crucial problem of the origins of growth, assuredly the primary strategic objective in the actual state of research. It was, indeed, the principal point of confrontation at the 1988 Flaran Colloquium and led to the articulation of diametrically opposed theories. For Pierre Bonnassie, it was essentially attributable to the peasantry, or more precisely to the consolidation of small-scale production (allod-holders or tenants) during the High Middle Ages.[5] The principal assarters were the small peasants. The final crisis of slavery was not entirely unconnected; fleeing slaves settled on waste land. The aspiration to freedom, the desire for liberation from the servile yoke, was thus one of the profound motors of growth. At the other pole, Pierre Toubert emphasised the role of the great Carolingian estate, thus undertaking an able rehabilitation of the pan-domanial theses which have been losing momentum, not to say in free fall, for some time.[6] He sees them as points where things crystallised, stimulating local trade by the circulation of surpluses and ultimately permitting small peasant production to assume its full role within the rural economy. So the spectrum of interpretations is wide. Without discussing for the moment the two most authoritative theses, I will offer only a few remarks on the subject of method before going on to consider whether the example of Lournand enables us to contribute to the debate.

Before a problem so vast, we should mistrust unilateral interpretations, based, in most cases, on an exogenous factor. I am thinking in particular of demography, the most convenient and also the laziest of 'explanations'. Certainly, the demographic approach is essential and indispensable. The number of persons is the best indicator of agrarian growth, and it is also a factor in this growth, providing that it is located within the chain of causality of which it forms a part; otherwise, we have only an illusory interpretation. How can it be imagined that shortage of food ceased to bear on mortality? What factor could have produced such a situation? Similarly, one certainly cannot deny, a priori and on principle, the possibility that improved climatic conditions might have had some influence. But it is still necessary to demonstrate their impact on grain yields in the temperate zone, and to establish precise correlations between the chronology of climatic fluctuations and the very marked fluctuations of grain production over the long term. This is very far from yet having been done. In the actual state of affairs, it is to be feared that this line of research betokens a refusal to confront the complexity of the endogenous factors, that it is essentially a sort of retreat in advance. It remains dangerous, however, in that it appeals to a popular taste, specialised or not, by giving the illusion of opening up new horizons, by investing itself with a scientific aura through its recourse to the exact sciences and, above all, because it is a gesture in the direction of contemporary ecological awareness. In sum, it is easy to 'sell', but it will be understood that such a criterion will not be given high priority in the orientation of our discussion.

The second methodological concern consists in clearly distinguishing the descriptive from the explanatory or, if preferred, the 'how' from the 'why'. Nothing is more dangerous than the gentle slide, sometimes imperceptible, from one plane to the other. It is one thing to assert the participation of the peasantry or of the great estate

in the process of growth; it is quite another to make this the determining factor. A micro-economic approach of this type is certainly
indispensable, but it remains insufficient in itself as long as the
behaviour of the economic agents is not related to a whole context
which calls for macro-analysis. We will attempt, therefore, to proceed
with the utmost caution, starting from a simple description of the
indicators of growth, proceeding to a description of the social conditions of growth (the role of the agents), and clearly distinguishing this
descriptive section from the concluding formulation of explanatory
hypotheses.

The third methodological concern relates to, precisely, macro-
analysis. We see, in fact, that growth in the High Middle Ages was
a major trend, plurisecular, affecting all aspects of society. It is
unthinkable that it was not directly related to the other major trends
then affecting society: the decline of the town and of long distance
trade, the weakening of the state, the changes to social structure, and
probably also cultural developments. To pose the problem of growth
therefore is to look for the precise correlations between these different
orders of phenomena. No interpretation which does not meet these
requirements can be wholly satisfactory.

The signs of agrarian growth

Demography

The most precious indicator would be the evolution of the number of
people. Can this be established? The demography of the 'dark centuries', as will easily be imagined, is obscure. It relies, firstly, on the
inventories (polyptychs) of the great Carolingian estates, which
record the number of surviving children (with what degree of
accuracy?) within the families of *coloni* and slaves.[7] So when we know,
for example, that there were two living children per couple in the Paris
region at the beginning of the ninth century, and 2.7 children near
Rheims at the end of the same century, we can posit an upward trend.
It also draws on physical anthropology; the steady advance of this
discipline has made it possible to determine with some accuracy the
age of the skeletons in the 'barbarian cemeteries' – when, that is, the
soil and climatic conditions have been such as to preserve the bones in
good condition.[8] This produces, overall, a pretty meagre harvest,

revealing at most certain features of the demographic regime: a very high mortality, in particular of infants; a low birth rate as a result of restrictions on marriage.

What does the cartulary of Cluny add to this body of information? Let us not ask of it more than it can provide; we will seek to establish not the precise number of inhabitants living at the beginning of the tenth century on the territory of the contemporary commune of Lournand, but only the lowest threshold above which this number was located. The calculation consists first of listing for a period of thirty-five years (which is thought to correspond roughly to life expectancy), from 915 to 950, the names of all the landowners appearing in the acts, either directly (as vendors, purchasers or donors) or indirectly (as owners of adjacent lands mentioned in the enumeration of confines); the risk of homonyms, it should be emphasised, is almost nil, so wide is the range of personal names. The list totals seventy-seven names, sixty-nine of them from the three principal settlements: twenty-nine at Lournand, twenty-four at Collonge and sixteen at Chevagny. The remainder are scattered between the secondary settlements (Merzé, Cotte, Mailly etc.). This is a minimum figure, since some owners might in theory escape our view, but the margin is certainly small, given the number of surviving deeds and, above all, the extreme fragmentation of ownership. Probably only some very small landowners may have slipped through the net.

The second stage of the operation, to enable us to progress from the number of landowners to the total population, is to allow for those who possessed no land: slaves, firstly, also the *coloni* established on the land of a master. A rough estimate of the relative importance of these groups has already been attempted on the basis of information collected for the end of the century, at the period when the masters granted to the abbey a considerable part of their property, in land and men. With more than 15 per cent slaves and 5 per cent *coloni*, the corrective required to establish the minimum threshold for the total population is of the order of 20 to 25 per cent, which leads to an estimate for the area under consideration of not seventy-seven but ninety families.

The final stage is to establish a minimal rural density. Here we encounter a further difficulty. The contemporary cadastral area of the commune is 1,150 hectares; it includes the whole of the old territorial units of Lournand, Chevagny and Collonge, but only part of those of Cotte and Merzé, the communal boundary having been established as the River Grosne. Since we do not know the exact area of these last on the other side of the river, prudence requires that we keep to the 1,150 hectares, on which there lived, almost certainly, at least eighty-five families. Rather than attempt to establish a precise number of inhabitants per square kilometre, since we have no evidence on which to base a multiplier for the household, based on average family size, let us confine ourselves to an order of magnitude, obtained, let us repeat, by default. On the limestone hills of the district round Cluny, at the beginning of the tenth century, we are close to a density of forty inhabitants per square kilometre. Whatever the margin of error, one thing is certain: this countryside was already well-populated. It belonged to that cluster of regions of high rural densities which includes the Paris region where, on the basis of the polyptychs, levels of population of the same order have been calculated.

The problem becomes more complicated when we try to move beyond one moment in time in order to estimate the population trend during the Frankish period, from the sixth to the tenth centuries. The textual sources, in particular the cartulary of Saint-Vincent of Mâcon, are little help for this purpose. Archaeology alone is able to throw some light on the demographic situation for the earliest period, and here we have the benefit of a fine study. I refer to the thesis of Henri Gaillard de Sémainville,[9] a work almost exclusively devoted to belt trimmings, for which he has established various typologies. His work is based, firstly, on a catalogue of sites of Merovingian cemeteries and, secondly, on the excavation of one of them, namely Curtil-sous-Burnand, a village situated ten kilometres north of Lournand (an excavation which encompassed 700 tombs). From the demographic point of view, two important results emerge. Firstly, the majority of contemporary villages and hamlets had their cemetery with tombs under slabs of the Merovingian period, which testifies to the stability of settlement (not only in the Frankish period but until today) and gives an impression of an already considerable density. More interesting still is the yield of the excavation of Curtil-sous-Burnand, whose 700 tombs extend over about 150 years, from the beginning of the sixth to the middle of the seventh centuries. Is it possible to deduce the number of living from the number of dead? The author makes the attempt, and in a convincing manner. It is first necessary to introduce a corrective to allow for the absence of the remains of children of less than five or six years of age, then to formulate a hypothesis as to life expectancy (of the order of thirty years).[10] By this method he arrives at a population of 150 inhabitants for this locality in the sixth century. Such a result has to be treated with the wisdom born of experience, since unknowns remain. For example, were slaves buried alongside free men? It is reasonable to think that they were, in view of the precocious Christianisation revealed by the tombs, but it cannot be asserted with confidence. Further, the calculation is entirely based on the hypothesis advanced for life expectancy, a hypothesis which clearly cannot be proved. These reservations apart, we could scarcely hope for a more reliable figure. Let us try, therefore, to interpret it.

The cemetery of Curtil seems to have served the two centres of population of the contemporary commune of Curtil (Curtil and Munot), very close to each other and included in a single territorial unit. It resembles at every point that of Lournand; the relative importance of the *cultum* and the *incultum* is the same, as is the place of the vine. The striking homogeneity of the whole surrounding rural fabric is apparent in the densities of population in the modern and contemporary periods. When, at the beginning of the nineteenth century, Curtil reached its population peak, with 571 inhabitants on its 811 hectares of cadastral area, that is nearly seventy inhabitants per square kilometre, Lournand had 713 inhabitants on its 1,150 hectares (in 1831). To use the rural density of Curtil in the sixth century, that is nearly twenty inhabitants per square kilometre, would therefore not appear unduly rash. We may conclude that the population of these countrysides roughly doubled during the Frankish period. Anticipating a later part of this study, I observe here, to put these figures into perspective, that densities of nearly sixty would be reached around 1300 before the appalling bloodletting of the end of the Middle Ages, as serious in the Mâconnais as almost everywhere else.

These figures may cause some surprise. They are, indeed, high, seeming to indicate that the major part of the demographic growth was achieved before the year 1000, the increase between 1000 and 1300 being only of the order of 50 per cent. We should not, however, draw from this conclusions of general applicability. We know that one of the distinguishing features of the period was the discontinuity of rural settlement, with the juxtaposition of patches of very dense population and empty or nearly empty areas; the overpopulated hills

of the Mâconnais adjoined a Bresse plain which was only thinly
settled. Also, certain specific features of the history of the Mâconnais
have to be taken into account. The Germanic invasions did not assume
here a catastrophic character. If rupture there was as far as settlement
was concerned, it happened in the last quarter of the third century, as a
result of barbarian incursions and social convulsions. The majority of
the Gallo-Roman *villae* were destroyed and abandoned at this period
– as was the case with the villa of Collonge.[11] Some areas were
probably reclaimed by the waste over a sufficiently long period for the
traces of the ancient parcels to be effaced, and only visible today
(fossilised under the new sub-divisions) with the aid of infra-red aerial
photography.[12] The low point was thus precocious, and it is reasonable to think that, by 600, the wounds had been healed.

Another special feature was that the Mâconnais was spared by the
later invasions. Neither the Normans nor the Hungarians raged here
and at the most it suffered a few Saracen raids, the memory of which is
perhaps retained in one place-name in Lournand (the 'chemin des
Sarrasins'). That said, these specificities of the region's history do not
explain everything. And while we should be careful not to generalise
from the example of the Mâconnais, it should perhaps nevertheless
encourage a deeper examination of the Carolingian situation elsewhere, perhaps leading to the revision of analyses tinged with a certain
pessimism.

On the basis of this hypothesis (that is a population density moving
from twenty to forty inhabitants per square kilometre), one would
like to go further, and establish the chronology and the modalities of
the increase and, above all, understand the demographic system (the
manner in which the three fundamental variables – fertility, marriage
and mortality – operated). But how? Let us first observe that a
doubling of the population in four centuries in no way represents a
'boom', even accepting the hypothesis that the increase was primarily
a fact of the eighth and ninth centuries. It reveals rather a slow rise in
the number of people, produced by a relatively stable demographic
system, producing only slight surpluses. This is all the more
remarkable in that, unlike in the 'feudal' and 'modern' epochs, there
were as yet no towns to fulfil the dual role of outlet and 'hospice' to
soak up the surplus rural population.

As to the components of such a 'system', we have information only
concerning the servile households, which, as we have seen, were

numerous (nearly three living children per fertile marriage). Can we extrapolate from this to other social groups? Certainly not; the master seems, as we have observed, to control the servile family, through the formation of new couples, as a function of his need for labour; on him, therefore, depended, the number of celibates, the age of marriage and, in consequence, the length of the period of fertility. We encounter here an original form of regulation, specifically servile in the true sense of the term, and essentially political since it proceeded from the authority of the master. This may well be the reason why the number of surviving children is here higher than that found within the context of the estate system in the ninth century (it lay between two and three). On the large estate of a great ecclesiastic or prince, the slave was, or was tending to become, more like a tenant, transmitting, with certain exceptions, a heritage to his descendants, so that he was subject to a constraint of a patrimonial order, as in the case of the free tenant or allod-holder.[13]

If further proof is needed of the co-existence of two distinct demographic regulatory systems, the figures themselves provide it. With three living children per couple, growth would have been more rapid, intolerable in the light of the economic constraints. The only tenable hypothesis is that of a regulator of a different type, of a social nature, within the peasant population, for whom the question of the establishment of children and the transmission of property was central. It is highly likely that marriage was already adapted to variations in mortality by the operation of various restrictions: celibacy or delayed marriage reducing the period of fertility.[14] Given the numerical importance of the allod-holders, this truly peasant system was clearly predominant. And it linked the demographic evolution of the village closely to the stock of available agricultural exploitations.

The extent of the cultivated area

These remarks lead us on to the second indicator of growth: the expansion of the cultivated area. While the formulation of the question is simple (how far had the occupation of the soil progressed by the beginning of the tenth century?), the answer is less so. It requires recourse to various sources and techniques: the texts, naturally, some of which refer to assarting; analysis of layers of place-names; examination of the division of land into parcels on the basis of the first cadastral plan and the plan-terrier of the abbatial lordship made on the eve of the Revolution;[15] study, lastly, of aerial photographs.

Each of these approaches has its perils. For the few assarts (five in the tenth century) known because they gave rise to a contract of *méplant* between a landowner and a *colonus* or small allod-holder, how many have left no written trace, whether because a peasant made an assart clandestinely or because a master simply used his own servile labour? Place-name evidence is more dangerous still. The presence of pre-Roman place-names clearly provides proof of early occupation. They are thick on the ground ('en boulemin', 'en pertuis-sandon', 'en doua', not to speak of 'Lournand' and 'Lourdon') in a sort of arc set against the heights of Les Brosses and the Crâ, to the west and south of the village of Lournand. Was this the oldest part of the territory? It is impossible to say. They indicate only that this is the part of the territory which has experienced the least later interference, a sort of zone of refuge, furthest away from the valley of the Grosne by which first the Romans then the Germans arrived to settle. Conversely, to the east of the *bourg* of Lournand, the place-names are of more recent date, but it is impossible to establish a direct relation between the age of the place-name (to the extent that this can be ascertained) and that of the clearance.

And what pitfalls await the unwary! Should we associate the *condamines* with seigneurial structures, as is often done? The *condamines* of Collonge are mentioned at the beginning of the tenth century, well before the appearance of the seigneurie, and they relate rather to ancient structures, since they lie close to the Gallo-Roman villa mentioned above. Similarly, the word 'essart' may equally well indicate a Merovingian assart or one made in the reigns of Louis XV or Louis XVI. We have a good example of this with the 'Essarts' of Collonge, situated on the confines of the wood of Les Epoisses, mentioned in 968 and 982.[16] They belonged to one of the dominant families, the Arlier, and formed a sort of micro-territory distinct from that of Collonge (the texts spell this out: *in villa exartellis*): so this was certainly a Frankish assart, and probably already old.[17] The same observation applies to the little clearings situated to the south of the wood of Chassagne (*in villa cassanias*).[18] So these are assarts which date back to the establishment of this Frankish family in the region, either at the initiative of the Carolingians, or even within the context of the *hospitia* system, that is to the sixth century. They were located beyond the sphere of operation of the rural communities. Consequently, the utmost caution is required in the use of place-name evidence; the dating is almost always uncertain, and the recent strata cause the more ancient ones to disappear more or less completely.

Perhaps more informative is the study of the division of the land into parcels. We will approach this with a view to establishing what it can tell us about the chronology of the occupation of the soil, by distinguishing with the aid of aerial photography a number of areas each characterised by a particular morphology (see Plates).

Zone 1 represents the most ancient system, and corresponds to the region where pre-Roman place-names have been best preserved. It extends to the west and south of the village of Lournand, continuing on to the heights of the Crâ, even beyond the territory of Lournand. Its characteristic appearance is found round all the old nuclei of settlement in the Mâconnais: an absence of main axes, a maze of little parcels of very irregular shape but in general fairly compact (squares, rectangles, trapeziums, triangles etc.). The majority of the parcels are surrounded by low dry-stone walls which served two functions (demarcation and stone-clearance), are of proto-historic date, and helped to fossilise the parcels. It remains, in fact, very close to its ancient state in spite of the regrouping of miniscule parcels which are clearly visible in the photograph. It is the domain par excellence – and this to our own day – of small peasant ownership. It resembles what English historians have called 'Celtic fields'.

Zone 2 occupies the central part of the picture, in a rectangle roughly joining the hamlets of Collonge, Chevagny and La Chaume to the village of Lournand; it thus spans the three territories of Lournand, Chevagny and Collonge. The absence of main axes again leaves an impression of confusion, but the parcels are large. This should be recognised as the result of the medieval regrouping carried out by the monks.[19] It should definitely not be seen as clearance of the eleventh or twelfth centuries. The farm of Blangue, for example (in the centre of the rectangle), was in the hands of an allod-holder at the beginning of the tenth century. Further, it is quite possible to discern at several points the latticework of the ancient parcels, similar to that of Zone 1.[20] The disappearance of the low stone walls demarcating the ancient parcels probably corresponds to the appearance of vast 'murgers' (accumulations of stones in high walls or heaps), such as that found between the castle of Lourdon and the church of Lournand.

Zone 3 is in the shape of a long band, oriented south/north, lying between Zone 2 and the ancient Roman road located to the east of the Grosne (the line of which has been followed by the railway). It includes to the south part of the territory of Lournand and Chevagny, to the north the greater part of that of Collonge, extending into and opening out in the territory of Massilly. Topographically, it includes to the west the gently sloping hillsides dominating the valley of the Grosne and to the east the flat valley bottom, liable to flood and devoted to grazing. The parcels are much more regular, and are here grouped around two orthogonal lines (north/south, east/west). The topography, less undulating than elsewhere, may well explain in part this clearer arrangement. But one senses above all the hand of the Roman surveyor. The two Gallo-Roman villas are situated at the centre of this zone, as are the *colonges*, or units of peasant exploitation, which very probably replaced them after the end of the third century. Unlike Zone 2, the medieval and modern period saw a fragmentation of parcels (at least on the limestone hillsides), taking the form of thin strips, which have disappeared as a result of a recent regrouping, but which can be found in the eighteenth-century plan-terrier and distinguished on the aerial photograph. However, this fragmentation was much less apparent in the meadows of the Grosne valley, since peasant property was there rare (the 'masters' were predominant before the year 1000, Cluny and lay lords after).

One final observation with regard to Zone 3: no trace of irregular parcels of the Zone 1 type, fossilised under the sub-division we assume to be of Roman origin, can be distinguished. Should we therefore conclude that Roman colonisation developed on uncultivated wastes which had not been the subject of an earlier private appropriation? Or simply that after two thousand years all traces of an ancient division into parcels have been effaced? It is impossible to tell, though it should be remembered that the first hypothesis has to contend with the fact that these are the most fertile and the most easily cultivable soils. Whatever the case, this was a sector which was intensively cultivated both at the Roman period and in the tenth century.

Zone 4, lastly, corresponds to the clearings on the edge of the large wooded zone situated to the east of the Roman road, related to the settlements of Merzé to the north and Cotte to the south. This was, as we have seen, the domain par excellence of the masters of the Frankish period, in particular of the family of Achard–Bernard. It is not impossible that the clearance had been started in the Roman period, but it is highly probable that the greater part of it (on particularly heavy soils) should be attributed to new arrivals of Germanic origin. It will be noted that the boundaries of the parcels loose their geometric rigour and that, for obvious reasons, these parcels have not been subject to a process of disintegration. Their compact, solid appearance thus remains close to its original form. A certain degree of dispersal of settlement, of which a few traces remain, was the corollory of the assarting.

Beyond this admittedly rather summary typology, the margins of the territories of Collonge and Lournand deserve a more detailed examination, since they display original features. But let us note at this point that the distribution of parcels confirms the general impression which emerges from the cartulary of Cluny: the larger part of the cultivated area had already been brought into use before the feudal revolution. The common model (usually elaborated on the basis of northern examples!), according to which large-scale assarting and the construction of the agrarian landscape are the work of the central period of the 'Middle Ages', does not apply here. In essence, to the west of the Grosne at least, this landscape was created before the third century. From Chevagny to Collonge, it is Rome which we still see before our eyes, and in the valley stretching from the *bourg* of Lournand as far as La Chaume, it is the landscape of Caesar's Gaul; on one side, a plantation economy of colonial type, on the other, hamlets in which ancient peasant communities had long been established. In the Mâconnais (and probably in many other regions of central and southern France), the superimposition of a substantial Celtic settlement and a dense Roman colonisation had resulted in a heavy occupation of the soil in ancient times.

To what extent had the cultivated area contracted as a result of the crises of the Late Empire? We do not know. Clearly, it was Zone 3 which suffered most. The walls, their foundations blackened by fire, of the Gallo-Roman villas were never rebuilt, their sites not even used as a 'barbarian cemetery'. Until archaeology turns its attention to their buried treasures, the only evidence visible to an attentive eye remains the scatter of fragments of *tegulae* (Roman tiles) brought to the surface by every ploughing. The fields which surrounded them were no doubt reclaimed by the waste for a while before they were once again ploughed by the *coloni* after a division into *colonges*, probably taking advantage of the relative calm of the fourth century. Their boundaries were still sufficiently visible for the parcels to have retained their geometric regularity relatively undistorted.

So the Frankish period must be credited with achieving the 'recuperation' (in a proportion impossible to determine) of ancient territories and the conquest of new agricultural land; this included the creation out of nothing of the micro-territories of Cotte, Merzé, Chassagne and Les Essarts (of Collonge), all on the edge of extensive woodland, which suggest the settlement, on the margins of the old communities, of a Germanic population by the *hospitia* system. Since we have no direct evidence of the scale of this new advance, we will try to assess it indirectly by examining the later waves ('medieval' and modern) of assarting. This regressive approach, necessary here, makes it possible to distinguish two waves.

The last assarting offensive began in the decade 1750–60 and continued up to the Revolution; it was in response to a sudden demographic excess. It can be traced in the archives of the *sub-délégation* of Mâcon, which drew up nominal rolls probably with a view to limiting the excess, and in the fiscal rolls which indicate the supplements of *taille* due from those who had benefited from the assarts carved out of the 'commons'.[21] The rural communities (Collonge and Lournand) had been the initiators, and they retained all their rights over what remained their patrimony. They entrusted the cultivation of the parcels to a fairly large number of 'labourers' and 'wine-producers' to assure them additional resources. The operation was relatively limited within the territory of Lournand, but on a larger scale in Collonge where the surrounding belt of woodland (especially the wood of Les Epoisses) was seriously eroded. These late assarts correspond to a sub-division of land into easily recognisable strips which are also found in the neighbouring territories.

The earlier wave was that of the twelfth and thirteenth centuries. Unfortunately, study of it has been made difficult by the many losses suffered by the abbey's archives.[22] It is most clearly visible at Lournand, in the central part of the Crâ, which owes to it the distinctive appearance of its settlement and land sub-division. In the cartulary of Cluny, the occupation of these heights seems to have been limited to the eastern part (on either side of the principal road leading from Cluny to Lournand) and the western part (recognisable by its subdivision of the Zone 1 or pre-Roman type). However, new settlement appeared, scattered over the plateau itself and on the steep slope dominating Lournand, in the area known as Saint-Claude; it owes its name to an ancient, tiny chapel which was very probably built in the third century, if we are to go by the vogue which dedications to this saint then enjoyed in eastern France. Its existence was brief; it did not recover from the great crisis of the fourteenth and fifteenth centuries. There is later evidence that no one was living on these heights in the aftermath of the Hundred Years War, and the bishop of Mâcon no longer mentioned the existence of the chapel in the act reorganising the local parish network after the end of the Wars of Religion.[23] But the chapel had, nevertheless, existed; its ruins were still visible in the mid eighteenth century, when it is mentioned in a notarial deed, in the course of the enumeration of the confines of a parcel of land. Further, an amateur archaeologist living in its immediate vicinity has exposed its apse in the scrubby 'teppe' bordering the road from Lournand to Saint-Claude. What we have here is a classic example of a medieval assart on seigneurial initiative (the lands paid rent to the abbey), creating new peasant tenures and producing a dispersed settlement. It is possible to see on the aerial photograph (Plate 3) the characteristic chequer-board sub-division of the land, with tiny units (visible in spite of the effects of regrouping), contrasting with the maze to the west of the Crâ ('en doua', 'en pertuissandon'). This late assarting was also classical in that it involved marginal lands with thin, stony soils, whose yields cannot but have been disappointing.

Is this the only assarting to be attributed to the central period of the Middle Ages? We should beware of making such an assumption. For example, between La Chaume and Collonge, on the barren uplands (altitude 390 metres) and in an extremely isolated position, there is visible an apparently interpolated settlement which may be contemporary with the one just described. Its place-name ('en forat') emphasises its marginality; the little chequer-board parcels adjoining it contrast with the surrounding parcels and are reminiscent of those observed on the Crâ. In any case, it was a very small advance, of limited significance (one or two holdings), and exceptional in character, since the dense network constituted by the hamlets and their territories hardly lent themselves to the establishment of intermediate settlements.

What can we conclude from these various approaches? First of all, one assertion is hardly open to debate: the increase in the cultivated area after the 'feudal revolution' was of limited extent. If a figure has to be suggested for the addition made by the successive periods of assarting, its order of magnitude would not exceed 10 per cent. We have therefore to abandon, in the case which concerns us here, the notion that agrarian growth was primarily a feature of the central 'Middle Ages'. By the year 1000, these territories were close to their maximum development. And though it may not be possible for us to apportion respective shares in the conquest of the soil to the Merovingian and the Carolingian periods, it remains the case that the Frankish period, taken as a whole, was decisive. It was not a low-water mark (as is still too often claimed), punctuated only by tremors foreshadowing the future, but a phase of agrarian colonisation which fully compensated for the retreats of a Rome in decline and pushed back the frontier of cultivation. It is hardly necessary to emphasise the correlation between this and the demographic hypotheses proposed above. It might perhaps be objected that it contradicts the thesis of the preceding chapter concerning the appearance of a relationship of a new type between town and country, and the dynamism which consequently affected both, but the paradox is only apparent. However dynamic the later agriculture, it remained a prisoner of the dimensions of the village territories, the boundaries of which, long fixed, could not be extended. Its finest fruits were harvested where the latticework of ancient settlement was looser and the possibilities of spatial growth were greater. We surely have here an example of inversion in development, the advance achieved by certain regions proving a handicap in the future. This could perhaps be verifed by a comparative examination of the average extent of village territories, calculable at a first approach by the distance separating, in a given region, the old nuclei of settlement. But, to return to the region of Cluny and even the Mâconnais as a whole, it is absolutely clear that by the year 1000, the perspectives of agrarian development were limited by constraints of an ecological order, which allowed only a sort of stunted growth.

Technology

There remains the third indicator of growth, in its qualitative aspect: technology. What level was reached in the tenth century in the countryside around Cluny? In one respect at least, that of water power, the answer is clear. The network of water-mills was already in place when the monks settled in Cluny. Indeed, one of their first concerns was to make sure of their control over them. By 916 they had obtained by the gift of a certain Adalgisus, member of a local family of masters, the mill of Massilly, a village situated immediately below Collonge.[24] The mill most immediately relevant to the territories which are our direct concern had been constructed in the hamlet of Merzé. Its complicated history is interesting in a number of respects.[25] Cluny had obtained this mill, too, by gift, before leasing it back, probably towards the middle of the tenth century. Then followed the disturbances associated with the feudal revolution, culminating around 990–1000; the mill of Merzé was destroyed (*desolatum et adnihilatum ob malorum oppressionem homininum*). The head of the most powerful local family, Achard, dignified on this occasion by the double qualification of *miles* and *clericus*, took possession of the site and rebuilt the mill, 'against the wishes' of the prior of the abbey. There followed lengthy proceedings beginning with an initial compromise (Achard retaining ownership of half the mill until his death) and culminating in the full renunciation by Achard of his rights. Possession of mills was, we see, something worth fighting for, thanks both to the associated revenues and to the social influence it procured in the neighbouring peasant communities.

Was this a rudimentary construction on the edge of the Grosne? Not at all; its mill-race and dam are mentioned. However, we have no way of knowing when these works had first been undertaken. Was it, here in the depths of the country, a recent innovation? We have to be content with two conclusions: the decisive progress in this regard was made prior to the ninth century, and water-mills existed, even in the absence of the great estate.

On the subject of agricultural practices and tools, we are less well-informed. The only firm information we possess is later. It comes in an estate document drawn up around 1156 at the request of Peter the Venerable, abbot of Cluny, by Henry, bishop of Winchester and creditor of the abbey, with the aim of improving the revenues from the abbey's temporalities.[26] The operation was conducted with a high degree of attention to detail. The various administrative units of the abbey's temporalities (the 'deaneries') were successively reviewed: the proceeds of peasant rents, of tithes and of the churches and barns of the 'demesne' exploited directly. The deanery of Lourdon, which encompassed many villages, including those studied here, appears in this precious inventory, so we have precise information about the techniques being applied. It emerges that a three-course rotation was practised, certainly on the abbey's own fields, since, we are told, fifty *sétiers* of barley and oats were set aside for the 'Lent sowing', and probably on at least some of the peasant tenures, which carried fairly heavy rents in oats, admittedly then commuted to cash. So what is generally presented as one of the major innovations of medieval agriculture (leaving the land to rest only one year in three) seems to have been firmly established in the mid twelfth century. This fact is all the more remarkable in that we are to the south of the historical border separating in so many respects (types of plough, crop rotations, types of tile, not to speak of juridical and linguistic matters) southern France (domain of two-course rotation) from northern France (domain of three-course rotation). What is more, the Cluny region would later join the zone of the two-course rotation. In the modern period, leases for cash and share-cropping leases assumed a triennial rotation only on the large units. Elsewhere, the wheat/fallow combination, that is an intensive two-course rotation, was the general rule. The *Statistique agricole de la France* (1841) provides final proof; winter corns were here overwhelmingly predominant.

How should we interpret this body of information? To what should we attribute the breakthrough of the three-course rotation in a countryside where Roman influence remained strong, and the horse was rare? To the monks? Or, before them, to the masters, the localisation of whose activities already hints at agricultural orientations distinctively different from those of the surrounding communities? We can only conjecture. What is most probable is that the monks found in existence, already well-established on the lands of the masters, the practice of the three-course rotation, and that, through the labour services and rents they demanded from their tenants, they contributed to a temporary increase in its diffusion within the peasant economy itself; demographic pressure then compelled the peasants to concentrate on bread-producing cereals, sowing them one year in two. One thing, however, is certain: the rural economy of the Cluny region had very early reached a relative technical modernity, of which other indications survive.

For example, the tenants of Peter the Venerable were obliged to perform four annual ploughings on the seigneurial fields, two of them on the fallow; they used a plough of a heavy type, clearly equipped with wheels and drawn by six oxen.[27] Nor, finally, was this situation confined exclusively to the abbey's demesnes. Analagous indications of precocious technical development throughout the Mâconnais can easily be found (the diffusion of the water-mill being a prime example). This justifies us in regarding it, without undue risk of error, as essentially an achievement of the Frankish period. Certainly, the transformation of agricultural techniques was not general. The wine-producer, for example, continued to use the techniques inherited from Rome. But it was a period when a variety of technical improvements took root, of which the two most obvious consequences were a greater mastery of water and animal power (liberating an equivalent amount of human energy) and a closer integration of pastoral and cereal farming. We are thus close to the high point, from the technical point of view, of an old agrarian civilisation, the slow maturing of which we should no doubt locate within a several-thousand-year-long perspective, as with India and China. The polyculture practised in the hills of the Mâconnais in the tenth century differed little from that we can see in operation under the Second Empire and even later. This was precisely because it had reached its highest point, and constituted a technical system which, while apparently simple, was in reality based on structures of extreme complexity: an equilibrium between *ager* and *saltus*, the reconciliation of the contradictory requirements of pastoral and arable farming, the combination of a form of production which was essentially family-based and a community solidarity which was indispensable to it. When a system of production reaches such a degree of internal coherence, it is no longer susceptible of evolution, except in the form of minor improvements or on the margins of communities and their territories. One element can no longer be altered without threatening the whole. Innovation is dangerous. The feudal system would, in fact, erect this principle into a theory.

On the one hand, a perceptible demographic advance, on the other an increase in agricultural resources resulting both from technical improvements and an extensive occupation of the soil, such are the two elements of our analysis. The reciprocal relations between the two phenomena are not in doubt. But correlation cannot take the place of explanation. At the end of an extremely interesting conference on the theme of population and resources held under the auspices of the Collège de France in 1983, where the processes of agrarian growth were discussed on the basis of societies very different from each other in time and space, Pierre Gourou made this point strongly.[28] Referring to the distribution of men and their works over the planet, he concluded:

It seems to me that for many others than geographers, the key to these distributions cannot be obtained by a simple 'techniques–population' comparison; there needs to be introduced into any attempt at explanation a third component which I would like to classify under the rubric of 'contextual techniques'. Whilst it is an obvious truth to say that people are affected in innumerable ways by their context, it is a truth too often forgotten. Between the production of the foodstuffs necessary to their survival and the number of people, relations are not direct, but pass through the intermediary of a context which favours or hinders an increase in the number of people. It seems to me also, as regards 'development', that the role of the context is essential; it favours or hinders development just as it favours or hinders production or an increase in population.

Let us now examine the 'social conditions' of agrarian growth, adopting the problematic of Pierre Gourou.

The social conditions of growth

If we accept the thesis which has just been proposed, namely that the take-off of agricultural growth was precocious, happening well before the year 1000 and the establishment of feudal structures, the following question then arises: what modifications experienced at the level of the structural framework could have provoked or facilitated this breakthrough? This is really two questions, inasmuch as our analysis of society has revealed the coexistence of two sectors of activity which, though not separated by an impenetrable barrier, were none the less quite distinct and seem likely to have obeyed different logics.

The peasants and growth

Let us start with the peasant economy. The allod-holders, as we have seen, constituted two thirds of the village population. Agrarian growth, in its demographic or spatial dimension, was consequently inconceivable without them; it even implies dynamism on the part of this social group. Also, from a simple descriptive point of view, the Frankish period was here a period of the blossoming of small peasant production. The large Roman estates dominating the valley of the

Grosne had disappeared, giving way to peasant *colonges*. Subsequently, we see not the least trace of a demesne system, nor even of large estates using servile labour. The economic fabric had become a tissue of fine mesh essentially based on the small family farm. Let us remark in passing that this was the first sign announcing the future 'feudal society', a point to which we will return. In the double process of disintegration and reintegration which characterised the transition from ancient structures to feudal structures, the disintegration developed from the top down (starting with the crisis of the state), while the reintegration developed from the bottom up, the first sign of it being the enlargement and consolidation of small peasant production on the technical and economic level (independently of any change in social relations).

It remains to understand the profound reasons for this trend – of which the 'settlement' of slaves on holdings was another illustration. This is a question of a singular complexity: what explains the efficiency of the family farm? Should we see it, in line with the Marxist tradition, as the effect of a 'correspondence' or an equivalence between a form of production and a level of productive forces? This hypothesis certainly contains a grain of truth, even if there is no justification for assuming a direct and exclusive relationship between the two phenomena without indulging in an unjustifiable determinism. Let us note only that a certain technical level has to be reached before a group as restricted as the conjugal unit can assert its autonomy in production, and so free itself from wider constraints and solidarities. This level had manifestly long been reached. Already, in the case of Roman agriculture, Moses Finley has emphasised 'the powerful attraction of the model provided by the peasant household' and explained in this way why the enlargement of the scale of the farm did not follow the process of concentration of ownership.[29] We see here an indispensable backdrop, a sort of necessary condition, but not the immediate key to the problem posed by the strengthening of small peasant production in the Frankish period.

The impulsions surely came from the new contexts in which the peasant economy operated. The first fact was the collapse of the political structure. The degree of *dirigisme* and sclerosis reached by the Late Empire as it declined is well known. The countryside had been its first victim. The financial burden weighing on it had grown constantly heavier since the third century. The volume of levies by the state has been estimated at between one quarter and one third of the gross product of the land, without counting the various exactions suffered by small and middling landowners.[30] This was an iron corset preventing rural expansion, even ruining the capacity for production (multiplication of the *agri deserti*) and causing, at the end of the day, the fall of the Empire. This event, which was followed by the more or less rapid disappearance of public fiscality, represented a major discontinuity in the agrarian history of Europe, as indeed did the reappearance of taxation at the beginning of the fourteenth century. The liberating effects of the cessation of a massive transfer of revenues from the countryside to the town have perhaps not been fully appreciated. Numerous rural exploitations which, in the earlier context, would have been stifled were able to survive. The decline of the state and its corollary, the decline of the ancient town, were the prior conditions for a profound respiration of the rural world. It was not by chance that the apogee of the countryside in the West was located in a long fiscal hiatus. The weight of the macro-economic constraints is in this connection too often forgotten.

But this was not the only result of the collapse of the state. Previously, it had structured rural space in innumerable ways over vast areas: by the cadastre, by its control over the circulation of goods, by its domination of the social hierarchies and, lastly, simply by the maintenance of public authority. The failure of the state paved the way for other types of structural framework. The second fundamental fact we need to bear in mind is therefore the growing role played in rural life by two structures, complementary, even inseparable one from the other: the conjugal family and the community of the hamlet or village. Some historians, notably Georges Duby, have correctly seen in the promotion of the conjugal unit one of the profound mainsprings of growth.[31] It had in effect become a stable structure, indissoluble, largely autonomous within the wider family, well-suited to mobilise its potentialities for labour. Let us add only that the affirmation of the communities went hand in hand with that of the family, and that both were dialectically linked to the retreat of the state. The community was nothing other than an association of heads of narrow families based on the need for solidarity and mutual aid in the exploitation of the village territory; it was an association which no longer derived from a common ancestry, supposed or real, but which was dependent on neighbourly relations and a territorial base. The history of these communities may remain plunged in a near-total obscurity, but it is impossible to doubt the central role they played in the Frankish period. I have already remarked how strong the peasant communities of Lournand, Chevagny and Collonge must have been to have survived to our day in spite of the later superimposition of new and wider structures (the seigneurie, the parish, the fiscal units of collection, the commune).

The study of the stages in the occupation of the soil lends further support to this claim. Before the year 1000, not a single peasant broke free from the solidarities of the hamlet to settle, for example, in some remote spot. It has sometimes been said that the 'High Middle Ages' was marked by colonisation of a dispersed type producing dispersed settlement and that the establishment of the seigneurie resulted in a regrouping of peasants under the wing of the lord, thus concentrating settlement and creating the village. The example of Lournand categorically contradicts this schema. True, if one confines oneself to the plane of settlement alone, taking no account of the social realities it masks, one might be inclined to this opinion. One might assert the existence in the tenth century of various isolated settlements (at Les Essarts in Collonge, in Chassagne, in Mailly, in Cotte etc.), the majority of which soon disappeared, very probably with the establishment of the monastic lordship. This might have been seen as the consequence of a deliberate policy of regrouping the population.

But micro-analysis rules such an interpretation out, saving us from a whole chain of subsequent error. In every case, these dispersed settlements were associated with masters who owned slaves.[32] Their social condition made it possible for them to live outside the hamlet; their separation was even a mark of their social distinction. Marc Bloch was well aware of this: 'We must be careful, however, to make some necessary distinctions. The term hamlet definitely implies occupation by a group, however small. An isolated farmstead is something else again, implying a different social order and different customs, based on rejection of the cheek by jowl existence of communal living . . . the peasants of the early Middle Ages lived side by side in communal groups'.[33] Peasant dispersal was no doubt a possibility wherever a strong political authority, inherited from Rome, had been maintained. Where this was lacking, the hamlet became the structural framework which no peasant would think of leaving. The basic reality consisted of a network of hamlets, each binding the conjugal units into a cohesive group. The more society lost any central power, the stronger the knots in the mesh became; hence the particularities of agrarian growth.

This took the form of an increasingly dense settlement of lands of ancient occupation, rather than the creation of new; the absence of a political framework and the strength of the tie which bound each family to its hamlet inhibited any venture on to virgin territory. Consequently, the expansion of the cultivated area was less spectacular than in the subsequent period, since circumscribed within the bounds of each village territory; it was no less real, and it intensified the disparities between areas of dense settlement and lightly settled zones. It was the imposition of the *seigneurie banale* or the castellan, that is the exercise of a strong authority over a district of some size, which would remove the barriers from the rural world on the plane of productive activities, as it did, as we have earlier shown, in the sphere of trade. It would inaugurate what we might call today 'land development', in particular by facilitating the mobility of the population, the very opposite, in fact, of confining it. It would mark the transition from one form of growth, purely internal to the village territory (which had, in fact, essentially exhausted its possibilities), to another, breaking out of the ancient bounds which had become too restrictive. From this point of view, it expressed an adaptation of the political structures to the demands born of agrarian growth itself.

The corollary of denser settlement was a more intense exploitation of the village territory. This was necessary as a result of the growing number of mouths to be fed, and possible thanks to the cohesion of the hamlet and the heavy investment in labour of the conjugal unit. It is therefore not surprising that there should have been reached, on the technical level, the culmination of the traditional agrarian system. It is true that we are painfully short of information on this subject, but it is highly probable that the close village co-operation which is visible later, particularly as regards animal farming (common shepherds) and the use of woodland (firebote), began to emerge at this period.

The last characteristic of this growth is more difficult to define, though it was probably the most decisive. It consists, to give it a rather abstract preliminary formulation, of the strengthening of the individual (or family) character of the productive process, a strengthening which was inseparable from both agrarian growth and the cohesion of the hamlet.[34] It was at the same time cause and effect of both: cause, to the extent that the autonomy of the family unit conferred on it a dynamic of its own, source of an improved mobilisation of its labour power; effect, because each step forward in technology or in co-operation within the community also gave to each basic unit a greater efficiency and, consequently, a greater margin of autonomy vis-à-vis the group. Agrarian individualism was thus in germination, drawing nourishment from the communal solidarities themselves. This was the time, it seems to me, of the slow, obscure emergence of the small producer, central figure of the future feudal society; in a sense, he made his entry as an actor on to the economic scene. Certainly, at the moment when we first perceive him, during the course of the tenth century, he still had a long journey to accomplish before he would be able to consolidate his nascent autonomy. He still had to gain access to the market to be able to dispose freely of the fruits of his labour; to forge a solid link between the family unit and the land necessary to its subsistence (paradoxically, tenure, by its greater stability, would achieve this better than the ancient allod); to obtain social recognition within the dominant ideology (the notion of *laborator* within the schema of the three orders was surely, in the last analysis, the prize gained once the long march of the small producer had been completed). In sum, it was the feudal revolution, culmination of the process, which gave to the notion of the peasant all its mental and social density.

But there is more. Without this evolution of small production in the direction of greater autonomy, it is difficult to conceive of the major upheaval which started at the end of the tenth century. I refer here to the rise of local trade, the birth of the market and the phenomenon which underlay them, that is the appearance of a new division of labour which encouraged country dwellers to specialise in craft or commercial activities and cluster together in the nascent urban nuclei.[35] But the new factor was not the separation between artisanal labour and agricultural labour in itself, since this had long existed. However, in ancient society the impetus to the division of labour came, in a sense, from the top of the social edifice, that is from the towns, whose function was political, where the authority, in order to meet the requirements of the urban clientèle, encouraged the presence of a 'secondary' and 'tertiary' sector, which it largely controlled or entrusted to groups with a more or less marginal status. In other words, the impulsions were in the last analysis of a political nature and had only a superficial impact on the rural world. Whereas now the impetus came from below, and specialisations emerged in the countryside. Some, in the case of slaves, should certainly be attributed to the initiative of their masters. But chance documentary survivals also reveal artisans within communities, such as the couple of shoemakers already mentioned who were living in 970 in the neighbouring hamlet of Varanges; in other words, we see a commercial production emanating from the elementary economic unit, the conjugal cell. The very conception of such an activity already implies a considerable degree of social autonomy on the part of the basic unit.

There was not, of course, a direct, mechanical relationship between this autonomy and the new division of labour. The one did not proceed immediately from the other, but rather found there terrain favourable to its growth. The clinching factor was certainly the construction within the context of the new seigneurial structures of a mercantile space which connected an urban nucleus and the surrounding rural district. However, it would not have entailed such massive consequences, that is the urbanisation of western society, if agrarian growth had not previously brought to maturity the individual behaviour of the small producer, by making him into an economic subject, no longer simply a component part of a group.

The small estate and growth

It is impossible, therefore, to exaggerate the role of the structural framework (especially the conjugal family/community duo) as a lever of agrarian growth and as a determinant of a certain type of growth, qualitatively different from that which would be experienced later. Growth was not, however, an attribute only of the communities. The description of its technical aspects has already brought out the role of the small group of masters. If, in the case of the communities, growth was probably essentially a result of the intensification of labour, in the case of the masters the dominant factor was technical progress and an increase in the productivity of labour. This is the factor we need to try to understand to further our study of the social conditions of growth.

Let us remember, first, the context in which they operated. The Arlier, the Achard, and others like them, were, relatively speaking, large landowners, even if their cornfields and vineyards rarely covered more than forty or fifty hectares. Their property was principally located in the Grosne valley and included the best pastures and some

fine stands of woodland; some lay on the limestone slopes, especially
at Collonge, where slaves produced cereals and, above all, wine. A
subsistence polyculture here remained the rule, with priority given to
stock-farming. We will not attempt to trace the boundaries of these
estates on the map; they were by nature unstable, constantly being
re-formed through the consequences of inheritance, gifts or exchanges. Is it at least possible to characterise or describe them with
any precision as economic units? The notion of 'manorial system'
would be wholly inappropriate here in its traditional distinction
between 'demesne' and 'tenures', linked one to the other by the labour
services performed by the tenants on the land of the master. What we
see, in effect, is a juxtaposition of small exploitations, mostly servile (a
few were entrusted to *coloni*), which were not, strictly speaking, either
tenures or demesne (the woods apart). They were 'small lordships',
according to both André Deléage and Georges Duby, and this expression certainly comes closer to reality, but it carries the risk of confusion with later structures, when the status of the holding, for the
moment embryonic, would have become fixed. 'Small personal lordships' would have the advantage of more clearly emphasising the role
of the servile bond as the cement which held them together. But let us
talk simply of 'small estates' or 'domains', it being understood that the
dominium was exercised simultaneously over men and land, and without losing sight of their internal structure, namely a constellation of
small units.

Within this context, the masters appear as entrepreneurs, men
heedful of economic realities; this is our fundamental finding. It is
based, firstly, on the initiatives revealed by the cartulary of Cluny.
When, for example, the monks entrusted the assarting of a piece of
waste land to an allod-holder or a *colonus*, by virtue of a contract of
méplant, it was surely an indication of just such an attitude. They were
equally displaying entrepreneurial qualities when they constructed
water-mills. It might perhaps be objected that their intention in this
case was more fiscal, even political (the concern to acquire control
over neighbouring communities), than economic. This may well be
so. Nevertheless, to build a mill was no small matter. It was necessary
to dig out a mill-race, hew mill-stones, produce the gearing, amongst
other things; the mill then had to be maintained and managed. This
did not demand an 'investment', strictly speaking, since the various
operations were perfomed entirely by servile labour, but it was still

necessary to take the initiative and to organise; this was the role of the master. He needed also to keep an attentive eye on the small units which formed his estate, fix the *servitium* required of his slaves, supervise the replacement of the servile couples on each unit and so on. The master was by no means only a warrior or priest devoting the majority of his time to activities of a public character; he was also an active economic agent, and it is hardly surprising if, in these circumstances, the small domain was the scene of important technological advances.

Nevertheless, this assertion poses a problem. In practice, nothing a priori predisposes a landed aristocracy to manifest a spirit of enterprise. Across various historical examples, it is more the exception than the rule. The Roman aristocracy, in particular, displayed a fine indifference to landed realities, which, as Finley has clearly shown, was a factor, if not the principal factor, in the technical stagnation of ancient agriculture.[36] The absenteeism of masters was perhaps an immediate cause, but Finley also identified a profound cause, deriving from the very structure of ancient society: this lack of interest resulted from the fact that the principal source of gain was of a political character; no fortune was made on the basis of landed revenues, all had their origins in administration or war, in gifts, exactions, confiscations, in sum, in one way or another, in princely favour.

The behaviour of the Frankish aristocracy thus represented a break with the ancient tradition. This key fact, were we able to throw more light on it, would enable us to perceive one of the mainsprings of agrarian growth. To invoke the ruralisation of the social elites, and their effective presence on their domains, would be not so much incorrect as inadequate as an explanation. The prior question is to know when this change took place; was it by the sixth century, under the impetus of the new arrivals, or only later? The example of Lournand, obviously, throws no new light on this question. Consequently, we will confine ourselves to a few general remarks of a problematic nature. First, it is unlikely that the rupture was early. The little that we know of Merovingian society shows that the 'powerful', whatever their ethnic origin, still looked to the public authority for everything, as in the past, except that the profits of war were now more important than the profits of administration. There was a difference of means, but a continuity of the principle which ruled political life and determined the status of the dominant layers in society. However, the expression of this principle was now based on the distribution of the landed estates of the monarchy, resources by their nature not renewable, unlike the fiscal resources of Rome. By the middle of the seventh century, under the Merovingians, the system 'cut out'; restored to working order by the first Carolingians (thanks to massive confiscations of Church lands and conquests), it jammed once again. One might therefore wonder whether it was not the failure of the distributive capacity of the state, through these successive malfunctionings, which gradually made it absolutely imperative for the aristocracy, in order to maintain its rank, to develop its local resources;[37] which it did by attempting to extend its domination beyond the little servile world and by rationalising the exploitation of its patrimony. The entry of the masters into the economic age would thus be the reverse of the political process which had atrophied the umbilical cord attaching them to the centres of power. This hypothesis, let us note, is compatible with the chronology of the economic revival of the West, indications of which proliferate from the second half of the eighth century.

However, the efficiency of this sector of production was not only a matter of mentality. It was also related to the structure of the small estate itself, composed of several servile units.[38] It enjoyed a first advantage in that it was based on small family production and benefited from its dynamism. The basic labour provided by the slave couples and their children was within this context. There was no large scale production requiring the mobilisation of large teams of workers and constant surveillance, no leakage of the product at every stage of production, storage and transport. The dimensions of these estates were small enough for control of each of these elements to be easy, and large enough for the establishment of complementarities, interdependence (transfers of labour by the creation of new couples) and probably some degree of division of labour. One of the slaves of Arlier, though settled on a holding, was a swineherd; Achard would appear to have had a miller; and there were certainly several artisans (a smith, for example) among the members of these servile families. And this perhaps constituted a further advantage enjoyed by the domain: the presence of a labour force traditionally accustomed to the 'mechanical' activities which had long been despised by 'free' men. A certain technical distance was thus established between the estates and the communities who procured from them their tools or relied on them to grind their corn; this technological gap signified dependence. In any case, the small estate happily combined, it appears, a valuable resource of the past (servile labour) and the valuable resource of the future (small production).

The large estate

The large estate bore no, or only a very slight, resemblance to what is customarily described as the 'great Carolingian estate', the economic inefficiency of which is now generally admitted: a sort of dinosaur, at odds with the new economic and social trends, even if, within it, vice did homage to virtue to the extent that the cultivation of the vast demesnes was based on the labour of tenants settled on small holdings. But, though poorly adapted, it was nevertheless indispensable. When the supply networks formerly maintained or supported by the state no longer functioned, and the market economy had not yet emerged, how otherwise could the requirements of the palace, various grandees and their entourages, episcopal *familiae* and the larger monastic communities be met? There was no alternative. The great estates were political creations, voluntarist creations, at least where the public power retained enough strength to create them. Adriaan Verhulst was, on this point, absolutely correct. I would add only the following observation: they were also creations in the ancient spirit. What was happening, after all, if not the assumption of certain economic functions by those who held, by one title or another, public authority? We find here again a form of the containing of the economy within the political which is characteristic of the ancient system. The state was certainly on the way to dismemberment, but those counts acting as local potentates, or those churches endowed with the privilege of immunity, were still the state (or fragments of the state, if the conceptual abridgement causes offence!), employing their own means. The difference between the great and the small estate was thus not one of scale but one of kind; the former was based on public authority, the latter on a social relation of a private nature.

The economic maladjustment of the great estate also needs qualification. It contained within itself the contradiction between the old and the new. It was maladjusted in its devotion to large scale production, and would be even more so when trade developed within the profound social fabric, rendering it less indispensable. But at the same time, it was penetrated by the new: it promoted small scale production on its tenures; it developed through its craftsmen the division of labour, and, lastly, it prepared the entry of small producers into the sphere of circulation by the rents it extracted from them. In this sense, Pierre Toubert was correct to emphasise the role of the great estate in agrarian growth.[39] It did, in fact, participate and it is undeniable that it was one element in the agrarian renaissance of the Carolingian epoch. It would be mistaken, however, to attribute to it a central or primary role. That would be to forget its contradictory nature, the rending, ultimately fatal, of a shackle riveted to the past yet dragged towards the future; to forget that the major source of its dynamism (small family production) was fundamentally alien to it and that it was only dynamic to the extent that this was allowed to exist. The argument soon runs into a contradiction, since it ascribes to this form of organisation imposed from above a structuring and dynamising virtue, when all the active forces emerged in opposite circumstances, far removed from the political, and precisely because they escaped the latter's constraints. In sum, we are at this point at the heart of the process of disintegration/reintegration, dominant trend in the transition from the ancient to the feudal world. The great estate was, in the short term, a brake on this process; it was even an attempt to take a backwards step. But in its other dimension, by the concessions it made to the new demands, it created the conditions for the later acceleration of the process, and the conditions for its own demise. On the economic plane it contributed to the growth of the small production assured by the tenants, and on the social plane, it was a place where the ancient frontier between free and non-free was blurred and where a new peasant condition evolved. It was thus doubly different from the small estate; more archaic as a form of production, more modern in social terms.

There is a final reason for not overestimating the specific role of the great estate in agrarian growth and for allowing the small estate its due. Empirical research has shown that the area of the former was limited and in strict correlation to the geography of power, which comes as no surprise. What was the situation elsewhere? Are we to imagine a more or less egalitarian society formed exclusively of a network of peasant communities? The hypothesis is perhaps conceivable for certain archaic margins of Europe, where the clan remained important. But elsewhere? It was surely the combination of small slave-worked domains and peasant communities which constituted the true essence of rural economy and society.[40]

Let us not leave the small estate without saying something regarding the other side of the coin. It was a flexible and efficient structure, but it was also fragile, and this for two reasons. The first was the constant danger represented by fragmentation through inheritance. There were, at Lournand, two estates of a fair size, but many others consisted of only three or four holdings. Their owners cannot have drawn much from them by way of surplus. For the families of masters, landed patrimonies failed to provide a stable or a sufficient material support. It was necessary for them to limit the effects of fragmentation or dispose of other sources of revenue; this meant that they had to maintain close relations with the ruling powers, the count and, above all, the bishop, on whom depended access to the various levels of the clerical hierarchy. Further, the estate was based on a social archaism, slavery. In this, it was clearly backward as compared with the great estate, where servitude lost its personal and arbitrary character. Over time, consequently, it was threatened from within by the slow upgrading of the servile world. At the end of the tenth century, this structure, which was also a transitional structure, in that it combined, but in a different way, the old (slavery) and the new (small family production), collapsed with the almost complete disappearance of slavery. But its role had been far from negligible in the economic, and especially the technical, development of the countryside.

At the end of this discussion of agrarian growth, what conclusions can we draw concerning the reality of the phenomenon, its origins and its consequences? As to its reality, there can be no shadow of doubt. It got under way well before the year 1000, in terms of technical progress, the occupation of the soil and rural population density. The agrarian landscape and settlement were then essentially fixed, later developments proving secondary. The burgeoning growth had swollen hamlets and distended village territories but without yet bursting out of the old bounds to feed the urban explosion or the opening up of new lands. And what we observe here was in no way exceptional; the densities recorded are, after all, of the same order as those suggested for north of the Loire by the polyptychs. Some historians (notably Robert Fossier) still paint the Carolingian countryside in gloomy colours:[41] no trace of technical progress, an unstable peasantry in shifting settlements, an atmosphere closer to prehistory than to the great agrarian civilisation of the central Middle Ages, a stagnant demography. In sum, agrarian growth was later, and proceeded from 'putting men in cells', from the 'birth of the village' – and from demography(!). For Robert Fossier, only the 'devotees of the Carolingian world continue to believe in the Frankish miracle'. It is hardly necessary to point out that one's feelings (devotion or phobia) towards the Carolingians are wholly irrelevant to agrarian growth. It owed nothing to them; it to some extent assisted them but it also transcended them, affecting the whole of the West. In the case of the Mâconnais, at all events, not only do we see not the slightest evidence to support such a thesis, but everything contradicts it.[42]

The question of the origins of this growth is of a quite different order. Only one thing is certain: there is no simple answer, no single cause (demographic or other), no false opposites (such as masters or peasants). A process of growth always has many well-springs. Macro-economy and micro-economy are inextricably interwoven, the economy in any case not the only factor at issue. Is the confusion impenetrable? Not altogether, since certain guide-posts emerge: the dynamism of small peasant production, the efficiency of the small servile estate, to which was owed, for example, the diffusion of the water-mill. These guide-posts direct us to the sphere of the structural framework, the role of which one then, more or less clearly, perceives. Small production would not have made the breakthrough it did without its close relationship to the evolution of family structures and its corollary, the cohesion of the village or hamlet community. Step by step, it thus becomes clear that the whole social structure was directly involved in such a process. This is not a theoretical postulate but a simple 'empirical' observation. It leads to one simple conclusion: it is impossible to produce an analysis of the process which does not distort it without locating it within a wider, more globalising, context; that is within the emergence inside a given society (bequeathed by antiquity) of a set of new social structures (touching all aspects of social life), which turned out to carry another type of growth, essentially agrarian. Ancient society had produced another type of development (subject to urban demands) before this was blocked by a paralysing hypertrophy of the state. After the Germanic invasions, the gradual weakening and fragmentation of the state were the dominant theme in the disintegration of the ancient system, and they had many consequences, directly and indirectly, on economic life. The burden weighing on the countryside was lessened, the dominance of the town relaxed. Above all, each retreat of the state favoured the strengthening of new forms of local structure which developed in their turn economic effects, which were also factors in the global process of the transformation of society.

One of the most characteristic aspects of this process was that the economy, from the bottom up, gradually detached itself from the ascendancy of the political; in a certain manner and to a certain extent, it became autonomous, which had incalculable consequences for the behaviour of the actors. From this viewpoint, agrarian growth and the emergence of an 'autonomous' economy were two inseparable facets of one same reality. That is why it is impossible to enclose this phenomenon within too narrow limits. Of course, once the problem has been relocated within a wider context, it remains to enumerate in great detail the multiple correlations which developed between the new structures, mutually strengthened them and constituted the underground reservoir which nourished their growth. Some of these correlations have been revealed here; many others should be brought to light. But let us not hesitate to say at this point that agrarian growth was first of all the direct and ineluctable product of the disintegration of the ancient world – as it were a sort of profound exhilaration of a countryside liberated from a ruthless embrace.

It was a product of, but also a factor in, this disintegration. A social system, precisely because it is a system composed of multiple internal coherences, is endowed with an amazing capacity to survive. It disintegrates gradually, suffers disturbances to its functioning and surmounts them by adaptations or recuperations of structures which emerge within it, but which, in the long run, accelerate its collapse. The process appears interminable; the system in crisis only gives way to other forms of organisation of social life when the forces for reintegration tend to gain ground over the obsolete structures.

Now in this process of disintegration/reintegration, the liberation of economic forces (affecting principally the rise of small production) certainly constituted the other dominant trend, in counterpoint to the weakening of the state. Its effects were felt through multiple social or mental mediations. Thus, the thrust of these forces acted on all the contradictions of the ancient system. It affected greatly and in a positive sense the servile condition (adding its action to the consequences of the disappearance of public institutions for the old free/

slave gulf); beyond a certain threshold, it affected the material condition of the free peasants, victims, through impoverishment, of their own advance (and simultaneously threatened by the decline of the public power); it even threatened the condition of the masters, in numerous ways already discussed. To the extent that the impetus grew stronger (and, logically, its rhythm must gradually have speeded up with the weakening of the brake applied by ancient structures), it contributed to the destabilising of the social whole. Let us at this point exercise extreme care; we are not suggesting here a primacy of the economic factor in the process, but only the existence of a dialectical relationship between two elements, the more active of which at the beginning was the political (the state, since it was the principal structuring factor of the ancient system, including at the level of social relations), whilst the thrust of economic forces ultimately became the dynamic element. This is another way of expressing the idea already formulated of an entry into the economic age.

Let us not, however, imagine that a moribund society dissolves spontaneously at the end of a long-term process. At the end of the day there is generally, under the influence of social forces, a disturbance, often painful, which finally makes way for the new. This was the case around the year 1000; it is recognisable as a revolution.

Notes

1 Georges Duby, *L'Economie rural et la vie des campagnes dans l'Occident médiéval*, Paris, 1962 (translated by Cynthia Postan as *Rural Economy and Country Life in the Medieval West*, London, 1968).

2 I leave aside here the English and Flemish examples which appear, at first sight, to contradict this assertion. In addition to the minor progress mentioned, it is obviously necessary to mention the existence of agricultural change 'on the margins', geographically speaking. It is clear, however, that this did not affect European agriculture as a whole. On this point, see Guy Bois, 'Population, ressources et progrès technique dans un village du Mâconnais (Xe–XVIIIe siècles)', *Des labours de Cluny à la révolution verte*, under the direction of Pierre Gourou.

3 Charles Parain, 'Rapports de production et développement des forces productives: l'exemple du moulin à eau', *La Pensée*, CXIX, 1965.

4 Georges Duby, *Guerriers et paysans, VIIe–XIIe siècles. Premier essor de l'économie européenne*, Paris, 1973 (translated by Howard B. Clarke as *The Early Growth of the European Economy*, London, 1974).

5 Pierre Bonnassie, 'La croissance agricole du haut moyen âge dans la Gaule du Midi et le nord-est de la péninsule ibérique', *La Croissance agricole du haut Moyen Age* (Flaran X, 1988), Auch, 1988.

6 Pierre Toubert, 'Rentabilité domaniale et démarrage économique de l'Occident,

IXe–Xe siècles', *La Croissance agricole*. Also his 'Il sistema curtense: la produzione e lo scambio interno in Italia nel secoli VIII, IX e X', *Storia d'Italia. Annali 6: Economia naturale, economia monetaria*, Turin, 1983.

7   J.-P. Devroey, 'Les méthodes d'analyse démographique des polyptyques du haut moyen age', *Acta historica bruxellensia*, IV, 1981.

8   L. Buchet and C. Lorren, 'Dans quelle mesure la nécropole du haut moyen age offre-t-elle une image fidèle de la société des vivants', *La Mort au Moyen Age* (Actes du colloque des historiens médiévistes français, 1975), Strasburg, 1977.

9   Gaillard de Sémainville, 'Les cimetières mérovingiens'.

10   No explanation is given for the absence of the bones of young children.

11   I would like to thank M. Guyot for having kindly shown me the report (1978) of the rescue excavation of the villa at Collonge (the site was totally destroyed during the construction of the TGV railway line). The building was burnt at the end of the third century and the site never reoccupied.

12   The archaeologist François Bange has discovered just such an ancient fossilised sub-division in a neighbouring village territory (commune of La Vineuse). Nothing of this sort, however, appears in the infra-red photographs of Collonge and Lournand. I would like to thank M. Bange for having shown me his photographs.

13   An alternative hypothesis would be that the move from two children (beginning of the ninth century) to 2.7 (Rheims, end of the ninth century), then to 2.9 (the Mâconnais in the mid tenth century) expresses an upwards demographic trend. The interpretation of these figures is made more difficult by the fact that they apply to different regions, and might also conceal local disparities.

14   According to the model established by Yves Dupaquier, which might well find here its earliest application.

15   Archives Communales de Cluny, plans. Musée Ochier, Cluny.

16   C. C. 1243, 1601.

17   Thorny scrub still covers what was very probably the residence of a 'master' and/or slaves, abandoned after the feudal revolution (archaeologists please note).

18   C. C. 1804, 1688, 1683, 1634.

19   C. C. 220.

20   The five principal 'granges' of the abbey accounted for 90 per cent of this group. See Archives départementales de Saône-et-Loire, Q 421, valuation of the abbey's possessions (1790).

21   Archives départementales de Saône-et-Loire, C 232.

22   There was considerable destruction of the archives during the Wars of Religion and the French Revolution.

23   Archives départementales de Saône-et-Loire, G. 378.

24   C. C. 201.

25   C. C. 2975, 3150, 3290.

26   'Constitutio expense cluniaci', in C. C., V, pp. 490–505.

27   *Ibidem*.

28   Gourou, *Des labours de Cluny à la révolution verte*, pp. 251–2.

29   Finley, *Ancient Society*, p. 153.

30   A. H. M. Jones, 'Over-taxation and the decline of the Roman Empire', *Antiquity*, XXXIII, 1959.

31   Especially in his *Early Growth of the European Economy*. For a recent review of the debate, see Pierre Toubert, 'Le moment carolingien (VIIIe–Xe siècles)', *Histoire de la famille*, vol. 2, Paris, 1986.

32 With the possible exception of the allod-holder (mentioned above) established at Blangue (within the territory of Chevagny), who seems not to have been one of the masters. C. C. 220.

33 Bloch, *French Rural History*, p. 11.

34 It will be noted that this also correlates with the evolution of family structures – not only the confirmation of the narrow family, but also the decline of horizontal solidarities in favour of vertical solidarities (the lineage).

35 This is a huge problem, which, curiously, has not received the attention it deserves, as if it stands to reason that a new social division of labour would be established.

36 Moses Finley, 'Technical innovation and economic progress in the ancient world', *Economic History Review*, second series, XVIII, no. 1 August 1965, pp. 29–45.

37 This hypothesis to some extent coincides with that formulated by Georges Duby in his *Early Growth of the European Economy*, where he associates the stepping up of the exploitation of the peasantry by their masters with the end of the conquests. The question is whether there was a more general (not only in terms of exploitation) emergence of new types of economic behaviour.

38 Though for other reasons, the decisive role of the small estate has been strongly emphasised by Robert Fossier ('Habitat, domaines agricoles et main-d'oeuvre en France du Nord-Ouest au IVe siècle'; also by W. Janssen and D. Lohrmann, *Villa–curtis–grangia; Économie rurale entre Loire et Rhin de l'époque gallo-romaine aux XIIe–XIIIe siècles* (Colloque de Xanten), Munich, 1983.

39 Toubert, 'Rentabilité domaniale et démarrage économique'.

40 On this point, I agree entirely with the views of Michel Rouche; see both his thesis, *L'Aquitaine, des Wisigoths aux Arabes, 418–781. Naissance d'une région*, Paris, 1979, and his more general analysis, dealing with the whole of Gaul, 'Géographie rurale du royaume de Charles le Chauve', in eds. M. Gibson and J. Nelson, *Charles the Bald, Court and Kingdom*, Oxford, 1981.

41 Robert Fossier has expressed this point of view on many occasions. His starkest and most recent formulation is in his contribution to the colloquium *Millenaire capétien* reprinted in *Revue Historique*, 'Naissance du village'. According to him, the birth of the village in the tenth century resulted 'from the taking of men in hand within the seigneurial context' ('putting people into cells'). The same thesis is developed at greater length in *Enfance de l'Europe. Aspects économiques et sociaux*, 2 vols, Paris, 1982; see also 'Les tendances de l'économie carolingienne: stagnation ou croissance?', *Nascita dell'Europa ed Europa carolingia: una equazione a verificare*, Spoléto, 1981.

42 Everything contradicts it, that is: stable settlement at a very early date, the strong cohesion of peasant communities, precocious agrarian growth and formation of the landscape, the lifting of economic barriers in the countryside (in the tenth century) which ought, at the very least, to correct the notion of a 'putting in cells'. But, over and above these numerous points of disagreement, I disagree with Robert Fossier as to the global view of the process. Whereas he emphasises the intervention of the lord and the alleged regrouping of men on his initiative, the model proposed here attributes the dynamism to the lower ranks of society (peasants, on the one hand, small masters, on the other); a dynamism which derived from the weakness of the political (the state), which in a sense liberated an energy previously checked and promoted new types of economic conduct, of a more individual nature. From this perspective, the establishment of the seigneurie was ultimately an expression of the determination of the dominant elites (or a part of them) to profit from this

dynamism by channelling it into the *seigneurie banale* and giving to their social hegemony material bases of a new type. These are theses not easy to reconcile!

1 **Collonge, the farm of Brocard (ancient Cluniac grange), and parcels of the Zone 2 type.** Detail of aerial photograph. Note that the regrouping undertaken by the monks did not eradicate the traces of the ancient parcels, which are still visible

2 **General view of Lournand in the 1950s**

3 **The *lieu-dit* Saint-Claude, on the Crâ.** Detail of aerial photograph. Note the contrast between the parcels of the ancient (Zone 1) type at the top and the regular parcels resulting from medieval assarting, below

4 **The ancient Cluniac grange of Brocard.** Detail of aerial photograph. In the centre, the ancient Cluniac grange of Brocard; on the left, the monastic regrouping has not destroyed all traces of the ancient irregular parcels

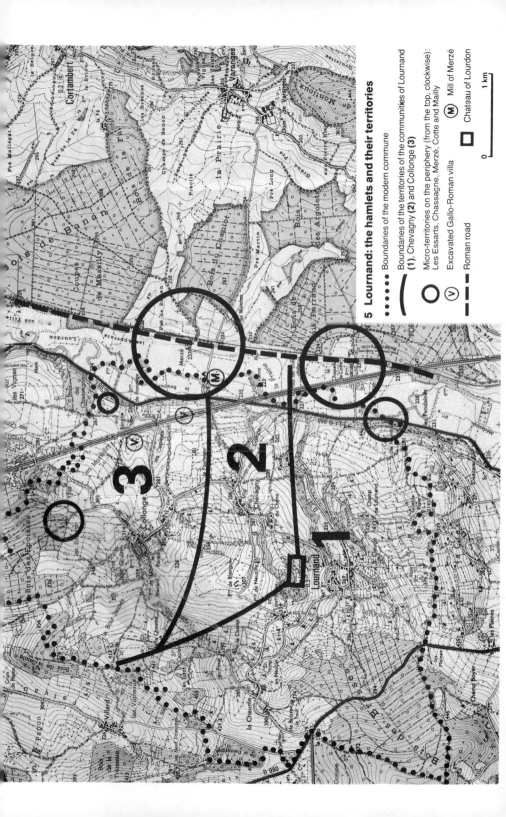

5 Lournand: the hamlets and their territories

·········· Boundaries of the modern commune

Boundaries of the territories of the communities of Lournand (1), Chevagny (2) and Collonge (3)

Micro-territories on the periphery (from the top, clockwise): Les Essarts, Chassagne, Merzé, Cotte and Mailly

Ⓥ Excavated Gallo-Roman villa

Ⓜ Mill of Merzé

☐ Chateau of Lourdon

– – – Roman road

0   1 km

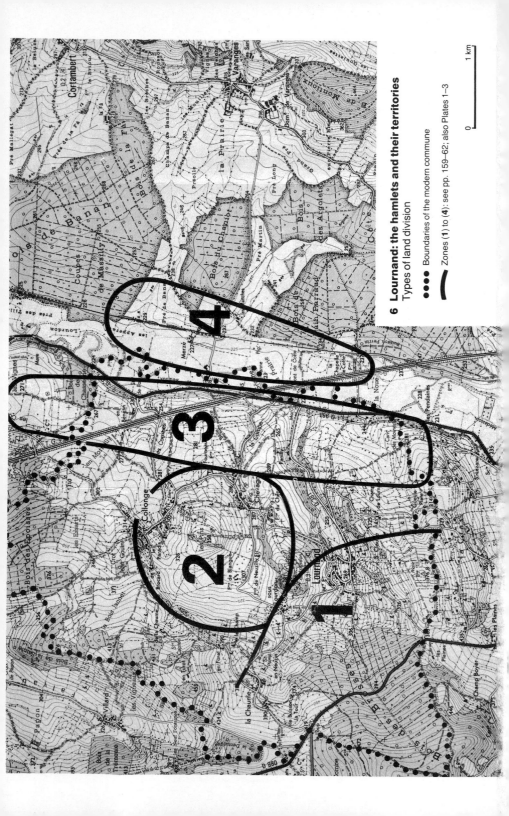

6 Lournand: the hamlets and their territories
Types of land division

● ● ● ● Boundaries of the modern commune

—— Zones (**1**) to (**4**): see pp. 159–62; also Plates 1–3

0 _____ 1 km

5
A revolution

We have so far given priority to our examination of social structures at the expense of a narrative approach. Had we not done so, we would have grasped only a sort of incomprehensible surface froth. However, it is now time to turn to the events themselves, as they unfold over time. In the Mâconnais, the dominant theme seems to have been the gradual increase in social tensions up to a breaking-point which signalled the collapse of the whole edifice. But this was obviously not the only region in which this drama was enacted. A detour is therefore necessary to place it within a wider context.

The revolution: a European phenomenon

The feudal revolution was a European phenomenon,[1] and its general character and unity should not be forgotten. It caused a major upheaval throughout the whole of the Carolingian West. A new relation of exploitation in the form of the *seigneurie* was substituted for the ancient slavery, now reduced to a mere survival, though certain elements of it were nevertheless revived and reordered in the serfdom of the succeeding period. New forms of political structure, which gave priority to personal ties, were substituted for the ailing public institutions. New ideological representations also emerged. In sum, the configuration of the social groups and their respective relations was totally redefined. Economic structures, lastly, also changed; trade, the mechanism of the market and a new division of labour between town and country breathed a new dynamism into the economy, and gave it a greater autonomy with regard to the political.[2]

The increase in violence

Though essentially one phenomenon, the feudal revolution had multiple concrete manifestations, in the form of scattered local upheavals with distinct chronologies. This constitutes, in fact, its originality as a revolution. It could hardly have been otherwise. Its dispersed character exactly replicated the dispersal of the centres of power consequent upon the decline of the state. As a result, there was no dramatic general rupture or symbolic event to become enshrined in the collective memory. Even the year 1000, though charged with a special religious significance (not wholly unrelated to the political and social context), did not fulfil this role. We see rather a period during which social life was disorganised over a wide geographical area. Its most obvious manifestation was a general increase in violence, beginning in the decade 980–90. Those responsible for it were the men of war (*caballarii*, soon called *milites*) from the social stratum of masters, with whom we are by now familiar. Their aggression was suddenly unleashed, against the peasantry and sometimes churches, in a crescendo of rapine and destruction. Obviously, their exploits have not left enough evidence in the written record to be traced in detail. However, their chronology at least is revealed by the prodigious efforts made to control them by all who exercised any authority, either temporal or spiritual. The impotence of the political powers was such that the Church stood in for them in the attempt to restore order, in the movement known as the 'Peace of God'. 'Councils of Peace' proclaimed series of interdictions which were sanctioned by anathemas; vast 'assemblies of peace' received the oaths of the warriors. The movement originated in the French Midi (Council of Charroux in 989, Council of Narbonne in 990), then gradually spread, reaching the Lyonnais and Burgundy (Council of Anse in 994). The violence, however, continued and the movement of the Peace of God experienced a new lease of life in the decade 1020–30, the years when the political disintegration was at its height, when, in the words of Georges Duby, 'things had come apart at the seams'.[3] Conditions calmed down only slowly and partially. But the worst was over. Thirty or forty years of violent disturbances was the price paid for the 'birth of feudal society'.

Cluny: an ideological laboratory

The Mâconnais and Cluny occupied a central position in the feudal revolution. The location of these Burgundian territories, at the point of contact of two contrasting political zones, predisposed them to such a role. To the north, beyond the Loire and Sens, in the old Frankish kingdom, the Carolingian tradition remained entrenched, and royal authority, buttressed by a powerful episcopate, continued to be exercised, more or less effectively, up to 1028, despite an increasing political fragmentation.[4] To the south (Languedoc, Provence, the Rhône valley and Auvergne) lay a 'country without a king', divided between many centres of power, and threatened at an early stage by the mounting anarchy. But most of all, the abbey of Cluny was directly involved in these events as a result of its programme of monastic reform and its success in this sphere from its foundation.

Already, the reforming ideal derived from a critical view of the corrupting effect of the surrounding society, and the increasing power of the monastery conferred on it very heavy responsibilities. Towards the end of the century, when the disturbances broke out, Cluny was already at the head of a developing congregation which joined together dozens of communities. Abbot Maïeul (948–94), 'prince of the monastic life'[5] and architect of this expansion, had become a leading figure in Christendom. He travelled throughout Europe, frequented the most prestigious courts, and was thus in a position to appreciate the scale of the problem the Cluniacs faced. They had benefited hitherto from the protection of princes; how were they to retain their independence, their property and their privileges when the political and social order was tottering on more or less all fronts? The monks had to find an answer to this problem, and it was an answer which necessarily involved them in activity beyond the monastic sphere, so as to intervene in the wider social arena. This was a decisive turning-point in the history of Cluny.[6] They actively participated in the movement of the Peace of God. Was this simply forced on them by circumstances? Only in part; they were associated *de facto* with the gestation of a new social order, obliged to find other secular support and channel in a lasting way a threatening violence. They became the theoreticians of this gestation. They advocated the transformation of the warrior into a 'knight', whose arms were wielded in just causes as defined by the monks (the protection of the poor and churches, and soon in Holy War); they demonstrated their concern for the peasantry, from whom they also sought support, and to whom they assigned a social function; nor did they forget to reserve a place for themselves in this new order: by their prayers they guided men towards their salvation, all the while controlling their other two functions, military and economic. In a word, they occupied a key position.

Cluny was thus the ideological laboratory of the feudal revolution.

In this role, furthermore, it was active at an early stage. The Cluniac social model was in germination during the abbacy of Odo (927–42): in his *Life* of St Gerald of Aurillac, the praise lavished on the virtues and edifying conduct of a member of the lay aristocracy already prefigured the chivalric ideal. After Odo, Maïeul, by to some degree distancing himself from the bishops, in effect turned away from the politico-religious structure of the Carolingian world. But the herald of the new society was probably Abbot Odilo (994–1049), or 'King Odilo' as he was derisively called by his opponents in the episcopal party. With him, the desire of the monks to assume responsibility for society in its entirety was confirmed in a developed and systematic manner.

Adalbero and Odilo

Let us pause for a moment at the years 1027–31, the very period when the social turmoil, beginning to calm down in the south, had further north reached the old Frankish kingdom. Here, another powerful voice was raised, in the form of a poem addressed to King Robert (Robert the Pious) by a bishop, Adalbero of Laon.[7] It, too, advocated for the benefit of the prince a social and political model. It, too, had recourse to a tripartite or tri-functional view of society; it could hardly be otherwise when, under the pressure of social change, the idea was surfacing on all sides. But the content of the bishop's model was very different from, even opposed to, the Cluniac model. In it, 'nowhere . . . do we find the men assigned the third function designated by a word that means "worker"' (Georges Duby); they were *servi* (by which he meant 'slaves'), and there was no justification, according to Adalbero, for exalting them as Odilo had done. For Adalbero, there were two dominant groups: the priests, with the bishops at their head, and the nobles, descendants of kings, that is the high aristocracy, quite distinct from those village trouble-makers who spread disorder and were wholly unworthy of consideration. Perceptively, however, the bishop observed: 'Already, peace is going adrift; the ways of men have changed and the order has changed'. Adalbero was nostalgic for the past; the old order ought to be restored, not by the indiscriminate mob at tumultuous 'assemblies of peace' but by the sole authority of the king, assisted and advised by his bishops. It is all there: the reference to the old servile relationship, still present in social reality but even more in men's minds, the defence of the Carolingian political system which had attempted to maintain the ancient structures by recasting them. We see a crucial ideological opposition between the two men, the bishop and the abbot, Adalbero of Laon and Odilo of Cluny; two systems of thought expressing the confrontation of two social systems, the one in decline, the other emergent, the ancient and the feudal.

The scene now set, let us return to our observatory and put aside the general aspects of the feudal revolution in order to look more closely at its manifestations, in the hope of thereby making some progress towards a reply to the questions left unanswered; once again, the cartulary of Cluny will be our principal source of information. What was the origin of this sudden flare-up of violence? Can we detect its immediate consequences? What was the attitude to it of the various social forces, and what, for each, was at stake?

Appearance of a dual power (first half of the tenth century)

The establishment of the monks at Cluny in 910 rapidly altered the local distribution of power. It introduced into the heart of the previous political structure a new element, a sort of autonomous nucleus, whose rapid development would threaten the stability of the edifice. Let us start by describing this edifice.

The fragility of the Carolingian order

At its base lay the three peasant communities of Lournand, Chevagny and Collonge. The fact that we know little of how they functioned is no justification for neglecting them. They were certainly alive and well. They controlled most of their village territory and had drawn a new vigour from the agricultural expansion of the preceding centuries. Solidarities had been forged in communal practices and the common possession of woods and pastures. A dense network of family relationships strengthened these solidarities, since the restricted circulation of men and things encouraged a strong village endogamy, in spite of ecclesiastical prescriptions in this sphere.[8] They were no doubt also strengthend by cultural practices; Pierre Dockès was probably correct when he suggested that village culture, with its many borrowings from paganism (in particular in fertility rites), dates back to this period.[9] In sum, the Frankish period was the time when the communities were confirmed as the principal structural framework of men in their productive activities. This was so twice over: the loosening of political authority demanded of them a greater cohesion, whilst the survival of public institutions, even in a weakened form, maintained the social gulf separating them from the servile poulation. They had thus acquired a real autonomous space in economic matters, and their members were still in a position to enforce their rights to their property before a public jurisdiction. A shadow, however, darkened this picture: the free peasantry was the victim of its own success. For the moment, in the overpopulated villages, the threat took the form of fragmented holdings and impoverishment. It led inexorably to entry into dependence on the powerful and, at worst, most at odds with their social values, to private dependence, the servile odour of which remained so strong.

The dominant social force at the local level was, in practice, represented by the group of 'masters', namely the seven families discussed above. They constituted the first level of power, properly speaking, or the local ramification of the Carolingian system. We should not, however, attribute to them direct authority over men. They possessed neither the powers exercised during the Roman period by the agents of the state nor the jurisdiction or 'ban' exercised by the lords. We should speak rather of a social hegemony coexisting with the fragile autonomy of the communities. It derived in part from a level of wealth which placed them significantly above the peasantry. Their estates, cultivated by slaves, put them in the rare but happy position of being beyond the threat of hunger, but also in a powerful position vis-à-vis their neighbours. A few 'free' men entered directly into their clientage, either as *coloni* or through the contract of *méplant*. Others, more numerous, were dependent on them to some degree in that they made use of their mills, obtained from them a few tools or simply sought their aid and protection. Their hegemony derived also from their family structures, from those 'horizontal' solidarities between blood relations and relatives by marriage which transcended the boundaries of the village territories and had a double function: on the one hand consolidating their influence over the communities and their authority over their slaves, on the other procuring positions in the clerical or military hierarchy. The maintenance of their preponderance (or the social reproduction of the group) depended first, as we have seen, on the exercise of social functions, whether in the service of the count or the bishop. This is an observation which applies equally at all levels of the aristocracy; for example, Georges Duby noted that the guardians of several comital fortresses owed their social position more to their office as castellan than to their personal wealth.

The local aristocracy was thus closely integrated into the Carolingian political order. It was just as much a power group as a class defined by possession of its estates and its slaves. Mainbodus, bishop of Mâcon in the mid tenth century, came from a family of masters of Ruffey, settled in this hamlet for at least three generations, and on the same level as the families of Achard and Arlier.[10] In other words, this aristocracy formed the natural social base of what one might call the 'Carolingian party', favourable towards the social and political status quo and with as its unchallenged leaders the count and the bishop, who acted in concert to maintain public peace within the *pagus*. Political stability depended on the cohesion of this ruling group, strongly structured by two distinct networks: a military network, of which the essential elements were the public fortresses (Brancion, Berzé, Lourdon etc.) where the local warriors assembled under the leadership of the castellans, and a more ramified clerical network, whose tentacles penetrated deep into the rural fabric. The institution of the parish was thus the principal local base of the Carolingian system; it assured a moral framework while at the same time being a source of substantial levies (oblations of the faithful, tithes). Here, these were shared between three churches: Cotte, Merzé and above all Lournand. This explains the central role of the bishop in the forces for tradition.

The fundamental weakness of this political system – the hidden face of the crisis of the state – lay in the fragility of its hold over the peasant communities and, in consequence, in its limited capacity to exploit the free peasantry. The hegemony of the masters was a source of some profit but was no substitute for direct domination. This problem had, in fact, been posed since the disappearance of the land tax in the sixth century, and would persist until the imposition of the *seigneurie banale*. The expeditions of conquest and then agrarian expansion had brought temporary relief, but the basic problem remained. The dominant social layer suffered above all from being unable to take more. The cohesion which it had demonstrated risked coming to grief on this point, since impoverishment threatened many of its members. Already, the local notables were casting covetous glances at the revenues of the parish churches and dreaming of imposing exactions or 'customs' on the local peasantry; the castellans entrenched themselves in their fortresses in the hope of maximising their incomes from them. Certainly, the unity of the *pagus* was still alive and well in the mid tenth century, and the traditional underpinnings of Carolingian power remained united; however, there were many indications of the imminent dissolution of this façade.

Social polarisation around Cluny

The establishment of the monastery was to precipitate the course of events by quickly leading to the establishment of a second power, concurrent with the first and an additional factor for social destabilisation. The novelty did not lie simply in the foundation of the monastery. Hundreds of others had preceded it without producing analogous social consequences. Nor was the substantial immunity potentially contained in the foundation charter, and subsequently granted, its cause. Religious communities of any size had long enjoyed privileges which conferred on them the attributes of public power; furthermore, in the case of Cluny, the count fulfilled the function of 'advocate' of the abbey and accordingly exercised supreme control over the free men residing within the territory of the immunity. Cluny was in no sense a foreign body within the Carolingian structures. Nor did the fact that its chief property was held directly of the Roman see imply either any reserve with regard to the bishops or any challenge to the role which had devolved on them, in the spiritual or the temporal sphere.[11]

Furthermore, the monks were equally well integrated on the social as on the institutional plane. They belonged to the top Carolingian 'establishment'. The majority of the abbots who influenced the directions taken by the monastery (Odo, Maïeul, Odilo) belonged to great families of comital rank. Their origins did not predispose them to question the basis or the structure of Carolingian society.

Nevertheless, the abbey very quickly radiated a special brilliance. It attracted a flood of gifts, extending its influence through the villages of the locality and beyond. In parallel with the expansion of its patrimony, it became a force whose appearance on the scene profoundly affected local society. We need therefore to consider what were the reasons for its powerful appeal. To invoke, as is generally the case, the high profile of its successive abbots is not enough, and easily degenerates into hagiography. The answer can perhaps be read between the lines of the abbey's cartulary; it is a remarkable fact that, throughout the first fifty years, the majority of donations came from modest allod-holders. Even in the case of sales and exchanges of land, the partners to the transactions with the monks were almost always members of the peasant communities. The reserve of the powerful thus contrasts with the generosity of the weak. Some of the masters followed the trend in the years 960–70, the rest became donors only at the eleventh hour, when, for them, the game was definitively up.

Such discrepancies in behaviour show that it was not only the piety of the faithful and the hope of salvation which were at issue, nor simply the reputation of the saintly abbots. Other considerations, of a social character, were clearly at work. They sprang in part from the peasant communities themselves: the presence of the monks appeared as an opportune counterweight to the pervasive pressure from their powerful neighbours. To enter into dependence on Cluny gave protection against exactions; furthermore, it was more honourable than dependence of a private character. But the attitude of the peasantry towards Cluny would not have been so favourable had the discourse and social practice of the monks not been so different from what they were accustomed to encounter. From the beginning, the discourse of Cluny had a very marked social tonality. The monks made daily assistance to the poor and the reception of pilgrims a duty. The fact was not new, but words were now effective. The desire to reform and purify monasticism by liberating it from the grip of powerful laymen sounded, whether it was intended to or not, like a criticism of the established order or disorders. It combined with the unease of those threatened with social decline.

Those who are richest strive to increase their riches beyond all reasonable bounds in order to satisfy their daily prodigality, to subjugate the poor and turn them into their clients. The poor submit voluntarily in order to be maintained by the rich, in order to oppress in their turn by violence, and thanks to their protectors, those who might not otherwise submit.[12]

These reflections of Abbot Odo in his *Life of St Gerald* reveal a clear awareness of the contradiction between masters and peasants, and a cast of mind which was certainly known outside the monastery. St Gerald himself was the model proposed by the abbot to the local warriors, whose way of life was less edifying.

At a very early stage, then, the monks went beyond their strictly monastic preoccupations to intervene in the social sphere. The evidence suggests that their success derived from an ideological factor or, to be more precise, from the conjuncture between an increasingly tense social situation and the offer of another type of social relations, conforming more closely to the moral values propounded by the monks. It has already been pointed out that the weakness of the machinery of Carolingian domination lay in the weakness of its grip on the rural communities; Cluny stepped into the breach with a master-stroke, of a moral order. It thereby won an important social base which strengthened its independence vis-à-vis the established powers. The humble thus formed the big battalions of the emerging monastic party. And the slaves must be added to them. Their entry into the sphere of influence of the abbey represented a qualitative modification of their condition; the 'servi of St Peter' were washed clean of the stain of servitude of a private character; they acquired the right of ownership. It is easy to imagine the direction in which their eyes would be turned.

To the ideological influence of the monastery should probably be added its economic and social impact on the surrounding villages, though this is difficult to trace in any detail. The abbey was initially a complex of modest proportions (construction of Cluny I during the abbacy of Berno), but the building works gradually expanded, mobilising a rural workforce. The abbey also attracted servants and craftsmen. A network of personal relations was established between the monks and the villagers of the environs; the opening-up of the communities began. We should probably not overestimate the influence of this aspect in the first half of the century; it was only after 970 that the sudden effects of the acceleration of trade and the circulation of money are clearly visible. We should see these new links as no more than a complementary element strengthening the solidarities established between monks and peasants.

All this came about without notable commotion. The guarded attitude of the local notables did not tip over into open hostility. Nor did conflict develop between the abbey and the bishop of Mâcon. The latter even granted to Berno several churches in the vicinity (Blanot, Jalogny etc.), including that of Cotte (in 929), and the monks had no intention of challenging the Carolingian structures.[13] They were content to consolidate the positions they had achieved in order to procure a stronger guarantee of their independence and they obtained formal recognition of their privilege of immunity in 955. Their power at the local level was based on an unchallenged juridical base. But it was not the institutional aspect which was the most important. It was rather the social polarisation which was emerging in the vicinity of the monastery. It is in this sense that there already existed a second power. In the long run, conflict became inevitable.

The conflict

From 960, and especially after 970, the course of local events gradually speeded up, to the point where a veritable social tempest was unleashed in the 980s. Before attempting to interpret this phenomenon, it might be helpful to describe it, by tracing the two most visible dominant trends: the entry of serried ranks of allod-holders into dependence on Cluny and the increasingly fierce resistance to monastic penetration put up by a sector among the masters.

A pressing hunger

The first development has already been discussed. The pace of grants of land to the benefit of the abbey accelerated. It was irregular, and marked by sharp surges (in 974 and, above all, in the three years 982, 983 and 984). At the same time, the nature of the transactions changed. Exchanges almost disappeared, whilst sales rapidly increased and donations rose to their highest level between 970 and 990. In a number of deeds, the indebtedness of an allod-holder, or a request for help and material assistance, or famine itself, are explicitly mentioned. There can be no ambiguity, consequently, with regard to these gifts. The peasantry was sinking into dependence on Cluny. Their prior favourable attitude towards the monks certainly contributed, as did millenarian fears. But economic constraints had moved into the foreground. Hunger intervened with a frequency and a severity not previously seen. The years 982, 983 and 984 were terrible; 994 was another year of serious famine. The problem therefore is to understand the reasons for the sudden worsening of the peasant condition, an issue to which we will return.

At the same time, the abbey came up against a social obstacle, that is the masters. This is hardly surprising. The arrival of the monks was detrimental to the masters in a number of ways. It showed up the anachronistic nature of the servile relationship; it reduced and risked even eliminating their influence over the free peasantry; it threatened their patrimonies through the incidence of pious donations; it represented, lastly, a rival power, conspicuously more prestigious, which penetrated the villages as none had done before. Just when their expectations from Mâcon, from count or bishop, were dwindling to nothing, the masters saw the ground being cut from under their feet in the villages. In such circumstances, they could ignore the monks, rally to their flag or, alternatively, confront them. All these responses were found during the course of the century, but with a clear trend towards a hardening of attitudes in an increasingly acrimonious climate.

The obduracy of the masters

In the early period (up to 970), the masters are conspicuous primarily for the modesty and the rarity of their donations. A handful of widows granted a small vineyard or a field for the salvation of the soul of their dead husband, as did Rodlendis at Chevagny in 936.[14] Another widow, Eve, showed greater generosity in giving a curtilage ('with everything attached to it: orchard, field, vineyard . . .') and a couple of slaves with their three children, in Cotte.[15] Here and there, we see a family of masters grant a piece of land and a servile family.[16] But for the most part, they remained wary.

There was only one real exception, the family of Arlier. They appear amongst the donors by 920,[17] made further gifts in 936, 967 and 981, and continued subsequently to display their generosity, including during the time of troubles (a donation around 1000, also in 1022, 1027, 1048 etc.).[18] Such generosity was costly and their patrimonies suffered. In the closing years of the century, Arlier and his wife Gundrade already appear as heavily indebted to Cluny and were obliged to sell various possessions to wipe out their debts. Notwithstanding, they remained throughout the period the most loyal of friends to the monks. This is revealed by the frequent exchanges of pieces of land undertaken by both parties, as a token of good will. Was this an example of a small aristocratic family whose piety, persisting from generation to generation, constitutes a reminder of the model of Gerald of Aurillac, earlier extolled by Odo? Possibly; however, the analysis needs to be taken further in spite of the gaps in the documents. We have already noted, when examining family relationships within the dominant group, the existence of two distinct poles around two principal lineages (Achard–Bernard and Arlier), and the hypothesis was put forward that these clans were synergies directed at the conquest of influence and positions of power. The impression (and it is no more) is here confirmed. The Arlier manifestly played the monastic card, whilst the Achard–Bernard (the most powerful family in the locality) played that of the bishop and Carolingian tradition.

This all bears a very strong resemblance to the rivalry between the families of Clergue and Azema in the village of Montaillou, three hundred years later;[19] however, there is one difference, namely that here the local factions had formed at a social level above that of the peasantry, though there is no way of knowing whether they had any repercussions within peasant society itself. The one thing which is certain is that the monks were able to take advantage of the split. Thus the ideological tidal wave emanating from Cluny not only swept along the mass of the humble, but reached the dominant group.

There remained, however, the elements who were hostile to monastic influence. They revealed themselves from the 980s, and in a number of ways: by the seizure of monastic property, by challenging earlier donations, by the imposition of 'customs' on the peasants who were dependent on the abbey, and by a variety of exactions. Their reaction was fierce, and violence simmered, reflecting a state of exasperation, a sort of last ditch struggle on the part of men with their backs against the wall. The chronology of these events is not always easy to disentangle, since the quality of the documentation deteriorates, so that dating is often uncertain. However, the main trends can still be established.

The first signs of trouble appear on the periphery of the area of Cluniac domination and are attributable to the 'masters' or powerful men of the locality. Thus Gerbert and his father Ramnald seized some monastic lands on the banks of the Grosne on the confines of Collonge, Massilly and Cortambert; they were obliged to renounce them in 986 before the abbatial jurisdiction.[20] At the same time, Ornadus and his brothers, sons of a certain Hildinus and heirs of Mainbodus, a native of Ruffey (who had, it will be recalled, become bishop), reclaimed everything which had previously been given by the bishop to the monks.[21] The affair was again settled in the courts and temporarily concluded by a renunciation by the three brothers of their claims (990). As in the previous case, these were young members of the local aristocracy who clearly felt that they had been despoiled and aimed to recover the land they had lost. The quarrel resumed some years later and led to blows and injuries to the participants. This time, Odilo, who had recently become abbot, had to resort to the comital tribunal, which imposed a second renunciation on the young men.[22] The disquieting element on this occasion was the spectre of Bishop Léotbald lurking behind the three rebels. An act in the cartulary of Mâcon provides proof.[23] It tells us that Léotbald had granted in precarious tenure the church of Château (in the immediate vicinity of Cluny, to the west) to the same Ornadus, and the churches of Brandon and Lournand (with everything attached to them, including tithes) to his two brothers. The opposition between a monastic party and an episcopal party begins to emerge. We may note in passing that Abbot Odilo very quickly reacted to this situation by demanding and obtaining from Gregory V a new charter of protection (April 998), which limited the ability of the bishop of Mâcon to interfere in the life of the monastery (an almost complete 'exemption').

The social storm

On the ground, however, the situation deteriorated. The year 994 marked the beginning of the exactions, properly speaking. Here, a 'servus of St Peter' was killed;[24] there, a horse stolen from the abbey by a member of the Achard family.[25] Yet we see only the misdeeds of which the abbey was the immediate victim. In practice, such acts were more general. Odilo denounced them in the spring of 994 before the Council of Anse (the Movement of Peace, originating in the Midi, had reached the area), which assembled, under the presidency of the metropolitans of Lyons and Vienne, many Provençal and Burgundian bishops, including Léotbald, bishop of Mâcon.[26] He demanded an oath of peace from the warriors and the preservation of the castle of Lourdon, crucially situated at the heart of Cluny's property. What happened next is less clear. At all events, the abbey lost control of the local situation on two occasions. The first intruder was a warrior, Bernard of Merzé, a member of the most powerful and turbulent local family. His exploits are not dated but took place between the Council of Anse and the first years of the eleventh century, very close, that is, to the year 1000. Amongst the evil deeds (*de malis*) of which he was guilty, two in particular stand out: he imposed daily labour services in order to strengthen the defences of the *castellum* of Lourdon (which he must then have occupied) and suspended the payments due to the abbey by its tenants in Lournand.[27] In sum, he 'held the men' of the

Gerald of Cambrai.[35] Both were responding tardily and in desperation to the discourse of Odilo. Iogna-Prat also claims that this schema had been formulated as early as the second half of the ninth century by Eric of Auxerre. That may be so; it proves only that, well before Cluny, the monks showed themselves to be more attentive to the social realities of the countryside. But let us not confine the progress of ideas to a sort of autonomous sphere, isolated from social reality, at the risk of losing sight of what is the essence. The decisive factor which gave its power to the tri-functional model and assured its diffusion was the social change which had taken place around the year 1000; further, these struggles lay at the heart of this change. In this sense, the model remains fundamentally Cluniac, whatever its antecedents.

What we observe, therefore, is an upheaval of major proportions, marking a rupture in the political, social and ideological order, not to speak of its economic aspects (the establishment of the town/country link as a direct consequence of the new order). It destroyed an obsolete edifice, eroded on all sides, undermined by profound social developments.

The driving force behind this movement was a faction within the aristocracy, or, to be more precise, within the high aristocracy in its monastic dimension. This was done almost despite itself. The sole concern of the first Cluniacs was to assure their independence with regard to the lay powers and to reform monasticism. However, this concern led them to develop close ties with the peasantry. There was thus an identity of interest (the peasantry feeling themselves threatened by the local grandees) and even an ideological rapprochement, to the extent that monastic spirituality coincided with the moral needs of the peasantry. From this moment on, the old order was threatened.

As often happens in such cases, the signal for hostilities was given by the champions of the past, by that local aristocracy, warrior and slave-owning, which formed the social base of the Carolingian system, but which saw its position being eroded. By unleashing violence, it plunged society into anarchy, thus compelling the monks to assume responsibilities in the social sphere and define a new order: the first draft of feudal society.

What is truly remarkable is the way in which the social situation erupted in the 980s. It was as if, suddenly, all the social contradictions,

village, to use the expression of the scribe. How long this continued is not known. But in the end, he had to withdraw and the venture cost him all his property in Merzé and Varanges.

This trial of strength was hardly over when another began, this time opposing the monks and a certain Maïeul, acting in his capacity as provost of the bishop. He was taken to task for his 'exactions' throughout the 'obedience' of Lourdon. Cluny took the conflict before the tribunal of the count in 1002 and won the case; Maïeul renounced the 'customs' on the monastic lands at Lourdon, Cotte, Varanges and Blanot.[28]

The worst of the storm had now passed.[29] The 'obedience' of Lourdon (soon to be known as the 'deanery' of Lourdon) was gradually organised. It consisted of a group of villages subject to the lordship of the abbey. The castle of Lourdon was its nerve centre: both administrative headquarters overseeing the various monastic granges and military headquarters assuring the maintenance of law and order throughout the locality. Warriors bearing the title of knights (*milites*) and swearing loyalty to the abbey were responsible for its custody. The abbot of Cluny[30] now exercised an unchallenged authority. Neither the count nor the bishop were any longer in a position to gainsay him; within the 'ban' of Cluny, the hostile social forces had been shattered, never to recover. As a further precaution, in 1027 Odilo obtained from King Robert a prohibition on the construction of any fortification (*castellum vel firmitatem*) in the vicinity of Cluny. In political terms, the revolution was complete; we will return later to the question of its significance, its impact and its social consequences.

Before doing so, we should emphasise the dramatic intensity of the two decades of the 'feudal transformation', since it was an integral part of the revolutionary phenomenon.[31] The chronological outline of events and incidents which can be deduced from the cartulary gives only a pale impression. They were twenty terrible years, with a paroxysm between 994 and the year 1000. The region around Cluny was convulsed from top to bottom. Long afterwards, on the occasion of a case concerning the mill of Merzé (destroyed during the upheaval), which the monks were trying to recover, the clerk drawing up the act still referred to the devastations and oppressions then committed by *mali homines* (wicked men);[32] the memory of that cruel period had been imprinted on men's minds. Between the time when the old order had fallen apart and the time when the new order had eventually been imposed, there had been a real dislocation of the social body, which had resulted in anarchy. Everything was interconnected: the pillaging of warriors out of control, famine and epidemic. The initial turbulence (982–983–984) had resulted from a first famine which had impelled a number of allod-holders to alienate their lands; the famine of 994 then inaugurated the most acute phase of the crisis. And, to crown it all, epidemic struck in 997 in the form of the 'burning sickness'. Let us turn here to a famous monk who, after various travels, had been received at Cluny, where he wrote his *Histories* before dying there around 1048:[33]

At this period there raged among the people a terrible plague, a hidden fire which, when it attacked a limb, consumed it and detached it from the body; the majority, in the space of a night, were wholly devoured by this terrible burning. People found in the memory of many saints the remedy for this terrifying pestilence; crowds thronged above all to the churches of the three confessor saints, Martin of Tours, Ulrich of Bayeux, and lastly our own venerable Maïeul (of Cluny), and they found through their blessings the cure they sought.

No one evoked better than Raoul Glaber the tribulations of that period when, in his words, 'the world order was then disturbed by various troubles'. No one understood better that this disorder and violence accompanied the birth of a new world: 'It was said that the whole world, with one accord, shook off the tatters of antiquity'; no one better appreciated the vitality which infected society once God's anger had been appeased: 'more than three years after the year 1000 the churches were rebuilt throughout almost the whole world'.

The rupture of the year 1000 was revolutionary not only in the violence it unleashed, but also in the nature of its participants. The description of events has so far inclined us to give priority to the role of those who occupied the forefront of the stage: the monks on the one hand, the warriors on the other, with, in the background, the bishop, proud guardian of the Carolingian order. But how are we to explain the victory of the monks, those 'lords without arms' (Iogna-Prat), over men who wielded physical force? Certainly, they benefited from a degree of support among the *bellatores*, some of whom were ready to employ their weapons in the service of Cluny. On numerous occasions, as we have seen, they even enjoyed the support of the count. Nevertheless, one would have to be blind not to see what was

the decisive factor in the monastic triumph. In the jargon of today, we would call it 'the intervention of the masses'. This implies the support of a sector among the military aristocracy, but above all, the isolation and defeat of the forces of the past. Lest this should be thought a mere abstract position, insufficiently rooted in reality, let us again refer to Raoul Glaber, who, describing the assemblies of peace, says: 'all over Burgundy, the great, the middling and the small made their way there'. The Christian people, as a body, was on the move; that was the revolution.

This may appear paradoxical, when one remembers that the result was the establishment of another type of domination, the seigneurie. But this type of paradox is by no means exceptional in history, it is even commonplace. That this participation took place explains, it seems to me, many aspects of the feudal transformation. Social storms of this type suddenly expose the archaisms of a society, and sweep them definitively away, social archaisms and political archaisms alike – in this instance, both slavery and the Carolingian institutions, or what was left of them. We have already observed that the slaves, at the end of a long progress, had reached the threshold of integration. What was likely to have happened during this tumult? They would surely have followed the trend. The answer lies in our sources. One after the other, the families of masters (Seguin, Anselard, Arlier, Elduin . . .) granted their slaves to the abbey along with the land they cultivated.[34] The page of slavery had almost been turned, the road which led to the tenure entrusted to dependent peasants lay wide open. And it is highly likely that many of these slaves came to swell the population of the *bourg* of Cluny, then experiencing rapid growth at the gates of the abbey. They brought with them their dynamism and their artisanal skills. The new division of labour between town and country also correlated with the feudal revolution, which we need to contemplate in its global dimension: political, certainly, but also, and perhaps primarily, social.

Archaic ways of thought were also swept aside to make way for new social representations. The schema of the three functional orders, which would become the feudal ideology par excellence, proceeded from the recognition of the social realities which were suddenly emerging; it was basically a Cluniac schema nourished by the feudal revolution. D. Iogna-Prat was correct to assert that the monastic schema preceded the episcopal schema of Adalbero of Laon and

hitherto contained, violently exploded. The peasants threw themselves into the arms of the abbey; the masters polished up their
weapons and prepared for battle. Why? We should remember the very
rapid changes which had affected the economic structures in the
decade 970–80: the birth of the market, the penetration of money, the
tremendous rise in the price of land, expression of the pervasive
inflation. We should consider the social effects of the unfreezing of the
land market and the appearance of subsistence crises which henceforward had a speculative dimension; in a society with a fragile
equilibrium, destabilisation was inevitable. It first struck a peasantry
which was already experiencing impoverishment, and speeded up its
dependence on the monastery; the repercussions of this development
threatened in turn the social condition of the masters. The spiral of
social crisis was in place.

The analytic approch has so far obliged us to separate the different
orders of phenomena, however closely inter-related they were in
reality. But the feudal revolution was a global phenomenon, a sort of
moulting of Frankish society, which rapidly cast off all the 'tatters of
antiquity', to use the apposite phrase of Raoul Glaber. It was also a
formidable liberation of social energy (a specific feature of revolutionary situations), of which the urban revival, the future forms of
agrarian expansion and the proliferation of Romanesque churches
were direct consequences.

Notes

1 The best approach is in J.-P. Poly and E. Bournazel, *La Mutation féodale, Xe–XIIe
siècles*, Paris, 1984; for the ideological aspects, see Duby, *Feudal Society Imagined*,
and D. Iogna-Prat, *Agni immaculi*, Paris, 1988.
2 It should be noted that the general nature of this social phenomenon is, if not proof,
at least a strong presumption of the unity of the underlying social structure.
3 Duby, *Feudal Society Imagined*, p. 125.
4 To use the chronology of J.-F. Lemarignier, *Le Gouvernement royal aux premier
temps capétiens*, Paris, 1965.
5 According to his successor, Odilo.
6 This turning point is analysed in Marcel Pacaut, *L'Ordre de Cluny*, Paris, 1986, pp.
104–5.
7 Adalbero of Laon, *Carmen*.
8 The extension of the prohibition of marriage within degrees continues to pose
problems. It should perhaps be re-examined from a political perspective. The
internal cohesion of the communities in practice presented an obstacle to the
politico-religious power of the Carolingians.

9 Pierre Dockès, *La Libération médiévale*, Paris, 1979, p. 127 (translated by Arthur Goldhammer as *Medieval Slavery and Liberation*, London, 1982).

10 C. C. 667.

11 See, on this point, Pacaut, *L'Ordre de Cluny*, p. 86.

12 Quoted by Pacaut, *L'Ordre de Cluny*, p. 86.

13 C. C. 373.

14 C. C. 461 (she was a member of the Arlier family).

15 C. C. 555.

16 C. C. 431 (935): Arnaldus and Aremburgis at Merzé (they belonged to the Achard family).

17 C. C. 227.

18 C. C. 461, 1157, 1158, 1580, 2144, 2331, 2429, 2430, 2555, 2556, 2775, 2804, 2967.

19 E. Le Roy Ladurie, *Montaillou, village occitan de 1294 à 1324*, Paris, 1975 (translated by Barbara Bray as *Montaillou, Cathars and Catholics in a French village, 1294–1324*, London, 1978, reprinted 1980).

20 C. C. 1723.

21 C. C. 1835.

22 C. C. 1989.

23 Cartulaire de Saint-Vincent de Mâcon, 392. This act, not dated, was drawn up between 996 and 1018; but it confirms the earlier donation by Léotbald to the three brothers.

24 C. C. 2254.

25 C. C. 2390.

26 C. C. 2255.

27 C. C. 2022, 2142.

28 C. C. 2404, 2502.

29 I leave aside the last troubles (1022–3: an attack on the abbey's estates by some castellans); it was a distant and muted echo of the earlier upheavals.

30 C. C. 2850.

31 The expression is used by Poly and Bournazel.

32 C. C. 2850.

33 Raoul Glaber, *Les Cinq Livres de ses histoires*, Paris, 1886 (ed. M. Prou).

34 The majority of these donations date from the period 994–1002.

35 D. Iogna-Prat, 'Le "baptême" du schéma des trois ordres fonctionnels. L'apport de l'Ecole d'Auxerre dans la seconde moitié du IXe siècle', *Annales-ESC*, No. 1, 1986.

Conclusion: from the ancient system to the feudal system

This book, as will have become clear, is neither wholly local monograph nor wholly general history. Between the two, there is constant interaction and questioning. The book is based on one simple idea – that the examination in depth of the particular comes closer to than it departs from the general, and is all the more necessary in that the general cannot be understood by the simple addition or juxtaposition of particular situations.

Applied to more recent periods, such a method would be, when all is said and done, commonplace. But for the Frankish period, the cards seem stacked against it. The sources, in the first place, hardly lend themselves to such an approach. To choose one village and use it as a field of research for the tenth century might appear to be tempting providence. I confess that I was for long uncertain, as I calculated the risks, whether to make the attempt. Nevertheless, to invert the gaze directed at a society, to orient the projector from the bottom up and not, as the documents invite, from the top down, was tempting. Every historian knows how the perception of a historical subject varies, sometimes totally, according to the observatory selected. Would this be the case here? The only way to find out was to press ahead.

This choice of method, like, indeed, any other, has its limitations, which have implications, in their turn, for the conclusions. These must be seen, accordingly, as above all in the nature of questions. A study carried out on such a small scale does not permit of definitive conclusions at either the local or the global level. It makes it possible to contradict or confirm earlier results, and examine critically certain assertions and arguments; for the rest, it can only produce a step forward of a prospective character: an indication of paths to be explored, the formulation of hypotheses to be tested, an invitation to a re-reading of the birth of feudal society, that is a certain reordering of the matter of history.

Reordering is perhaps the key word. Let us not see it as an objective easy to attain; it is a horizon prompt to dissolve just when one feels to be getting close. Why, in that case, pursue such a chimera? Because it is a utopia which is both motivating and stimulating; it obliges the historian to concentrate on the search for correlations between the most diverse phenomena, to be concerned less with one subject in isolation than with the links which connect it to others; it presupposes the rationality of the processes which transform societies; it is, finally, no more than the reasonable requirement without which the historian's craft makes little sense. So we must keep to our course, whatever the cost.

This is, however, far from easy to do. Firstly, because of the pitfalls inherent in such an approach: to depart from empiricism inevitably carries the risk of loosing contact with reality; a model cannot be outlined without a degree of distorting schematisation. The path between empiricism and speculation is an extremely narrow one; at every step, perils lie in wait. Furthermore, the current historiographic conjuncture (to put it mildly) renders such a course more difficult than ever to pursue. It is dominated by two tendencies which, each in its own way, reject the very principle of such a recomposition.

There is first the traditional approach. It is not without its merits: a tradition of learning directly descended from the patient and dedicated scholars of the past, which has made no small contribution to the solid reputation of the French historical school. However, its frameworks of thought are immutable: the notion of the 'Middle Ages' remains strongly entrenched, 'feudal society' is still defined as a society based on the fief. To depart from these frameworks is, in its eyes, to depart from the discipline of history, to enter the alien world of theory. To study another aspect of the feudal system, to suppose the existence of social systems encompassing at one and the same time the economic, the social and the political, is to engage in a type of exercise which has not yet won acceptance in a world where research is still oriented towards cloistered erudition.

The other tendency ought to be more open to a renewal of the problematic. It declares itself, insistently, not to say to excess, to be the champion of a 'new history'. It proposes to enlarge the horizons of the historian, to integrate the contributions of the other social sciences, and it has undeniably played its part in sweeping away the dust from a discipline which was in dire need of it. But, for reasons which we cannot go into here, and which probably derive from strategies determined by media considerations or ideology, it turns its back on globalising perspectives and becomes a 'fragmented history', a 'history in bits and pieces'.[1] The exoticism of such and such a particular subject (in relation to the preoccupations of the moment) and the rather demagogic rejection of an 'economism' which was, it is true, pervasive and stifling, are, in the end, the principal contributions of its 'modernity', and they are not always wholly convincing. It ought not to delude for long, but it looms over the orientation of research. It may be without negative consequences in the field of contemporary history, since the identification of the societies at issue poses less of a problem, but its repercussions are more disturbing in the field of pre-capitalist societies, where everything remains to be done in this regard.

To continue to aim at a globalising history signifies, in the present context, a refusal of the false alternatives offered by an archaic empiricism and a somewhat meretricious modernity, in the know-ledge that these do not conceal simple or trivial quarrels between schools or coteries but reflect the most profound divisions, since history, like the other social sciences, breathes to the same rhythm as contemporary society. This detour, whose length and ponderousness may perhaps be excused, was necessary to explain and justify the twofold choice which underlies the presentation of our conclusions: steadiness of purpose, on the one hand, our objective continuing to be a better understanding of the transition from ancient society to feudal society, taken as a whole; prudence, on the other, by making a gradual progress from the more to the less certain, by examining in succession the partial problematics, one more central problematic and, finally, their conceptual implications.

Partial problematics

These can be briefly described, since they cover (this was, indeed, the principle behind the plan adopted) the five propositions developed in the five preceding chapters.

Firstly, Frankish society remained a slave-based society and belonged, from this perspective, to the family of ancient societies. This proposition contradicts the assumption that slavery had given way to a new juridical or social condition (serfdom), while fully accepting that what survived was an 'ameliorated slavery' (the formula is that of Michel Rouche), and that the slave was primarily a slave of petty production, installed with his family on a plot of land; this last aspect is crucial, since it carried within it the seeds of the eventual disappearance of slavery, inasmuch as it conferred on the slave a certain autonomy, which set in train his social promotion.

The principal element of the proposition must, therefore, be qualified. Slavery was most rigorously maintained on the 'small estate', which we assume to have been a structure of major importance, involving a far larger number of persons than the 'large estate'. Why was slavery better preserved here than elsewhere? Quite simply, because the owners of small estates did not dispose of sufficient authority of a political nature (comparable to that of a count or bishop) to impose themselves on free men and demand their services. They could exert only authority of a private character over the families they owned; so they exploited this to the full, right up to the feudal revolution. Herein lay the principal forces for social conservatism.

Elsewhere, on the large estates of the high aristocracy, civil or religious, things happened differently. Slaves and free peasants lived side by side; their condition became increasingly similar, sometimes merged, and mixed marriages took place. They were thus crucibles in which a new peasant status was forged, precursory sign of a 'social recomposition'. Let us keep in mind this contradictory aspect of the process and, above all, let us not succumb to 'polyptychomania', since the great estate was not nearly so important as has long been assumed.

Secondly, Frankish society, like ancient society, rested on three pillars. The idea of two antagonistic classes is here inadequate; the principal actors on the social scene consisted of an aristocracy, itself very hierarchised, slaves and communities of free peasants. The dominant social class therefore resembled the ancient aristocracy more closely than the future feudal aristocracy, even if certain features characteristic of the latter (militarisation and clericalisation) were already clearly visible. It still owed its hegemony to the possession of slaves and kept its eyes firmly fixed on the profits dispensed by the public power, as had previously been the case. However, in this form, it was a class doomed by the irreversible decline of the state apparatus from which it had hitherto drawn the best part of its resources. It was impossible for it to recover the ground which had been lost. The drying-up of public resources was a cumulative process; it meant a reduction of the means necessary to control rural communities which were livelier, more numerous and more prosperous. The conquests had been an expedient of only limited impact. The Carolingian revival represented the last attempt to reverse the course of events, to put back on its feet a central power, and restore its distributive function (by means of conquests, confiscations of Church property and the institution of tithes). It was a vain attempt which, as we know, was to precipitate the ruin of the state and eventually result in the disintegration of the ruling class: rebellion among its lower elements, suffering social decline, and a split within the high aristocracy between those upholding the traditional political order and those promoting a new order. The feudal revolution was the consequence; it established an aristocracy of a new type, whose domination extended over the whole of the peasantry (and no longer over only the servile sector), thanks to the seizure, within a restricted territorial context, of the old public power. It depended henceforward on the revenues from the *ban* and on the rents levied on peasant tenures. In this sense, it was truly a new social class, a feudal aristocracy, qualitatively different from what had preceded it, even if most of its members came from it.

The free peasantry, like all voiceless classes, has been, from the historical point of view, the victim of its silence. Nevertheless, despite the obscurity of the sources, we can detect a growth in its numbers, in its cohesion, in its technical efficiency and even, in a religious sense, in its social consciousness. By this very fact, it made a powerful contribution to the destabilisation of the old order. But, weakened by the growth of which it was the vehicle, threatened by the aggression of the local grandees, it also played a part in the establishment of the new order. It then disappeared as such, to merge into a class of dependent peasants or tenants, broadly unified.

Before and after the year 1000 then, there existed two, sharply differentiated, sets of classes, one of the ancient type, the other feudal.

Our third proposition relates to trade and town/country relations: the latter remained of the same nature as in ancient society. The relationship was unilateral, a relationship of domination and exploitation, but (and this was what was new) it was steadily growing weaker. This phenomenon simultaneously set in motion the decline of the town, the ruralisation of society and the rise of the countryside. To connect the feudal system or feudalism with ruralisation is a nonsense; it was the malfunctioning of ancient society which was its cause. Conversely, the new local dominations resulting from the feudal revolution speeded up the rise of local trade and established town/ country relations of a new type, based on reciprocity, though the dominance of the town did not, for all that, disappear. The feudal system thus carried within it, from the beginning, the seeds of the commercial revival. It was fundamentally mercantile, much more so (despite certain appearances) than ancient society; it very early made room for a merchant class which was wholly integrated into the feudal order and no longer marginalised as it had previously been. Finally, by introducing the mechanism of the market at the very base of society, it conferred on the economy a new autonomy; it loosened, in so doing, the political corset which had constrained it.

Fourthly, agrarian growth was a central historical phenomenon of Frankish history. It benefited from the relaxation of the urban and fiscal grip, drew strength from the reinforcement of the conjugal unit and village solidarities, and accompanied the progress of small-scale production within the framework of the peasant holding and, even more, within the framework of the small estate, which played a decisive role on the technical level. Since the reality of this growth is hardly open to doubt, attention should be concentrated on its many consequences. It accentuated the fragility of the structural framework of the Carolingian world. Above all, it transformed the social land-scape, rendering the servile relationship more obsolete, thus enhanc-ing the importance of the peasantry. In this regard, however, we still need to take account of the presence of contradictory effects; a factor for the promotion of the peasantry, it became, at a certain stage in agrarian development, a threat to it (through the fragmentation of holdings and the impoverishment of people). On the economic plane, lastly, it created the conditions for a revival of trade (in a form initially intra-rural) and a more developed social division of labour. It is not by chance that the feudal revolution took place within a context of growth (analagous examples spring easily to mind). It laid bare the social archaisms, it engendered social decline and uncertainty for some, hope and acquisitiveness for others; it was by its nature destabilising.

Let us consider, for example, the case of Abbot Odilo, theoretician of the new society. Attentive, like many monks, to agrarian realities, he quite simply grasped that he could base the prosperity of his monastery on the construction of a local economic power on condi-tion that he was careful of and protected the producers, in short, by not killing the goose that laid the golden egg. His thinking was the direct product of a period of agrarian growth. It contrasted with the blindness of the old bishops in the Carolingian tradition, for whom nothing rivalled in importance the established political order and the authority of which they regarded themselves to be the natural guarantors. There was, in fact, an emergence of the economic in the face of the political.

Our fifth and last proposition is that the Frankish period culminated in a rupture. There was no gentle progress by imperceptible transitions from one situation to another. There was a drastic upheaval, affecting all aspects of social life: a new distribution of power, a new relation of exploitation (the seigneurie), new economic mechanisms (the irruption of the market), and a new social and political ideology. If the word revolution means anything, it could hardly find a better application.

Each of these propositions has its own justifications. But there are also close correlations between them. At this point, to conform to the programme outlined above requires that we stand back a little from these correlations in order to seek for the articulations which connect them and to refine the problematic. Inevitably, the degree of supposition increases; the project becomes more perilous, but it is nevertheless essential.

The central problematic

Its formulation will be organised around three concepts: structure, process and rupture. Our first proposition is that there existed two sets of structures, each both coherent and distinct; one was directly inherited from Antiquity, the other born of the feudal revolution. Each set was complete, extending to all aspects of social life, and irreducible to any particular 'instance' (economic, political etc.). In the case of the former, the principal features of the 'ancient' system as revealed by the work of Moses Finley will have been recognised. There are the same social characteristics, namely an aristocracy of power, a class of free men and slaves. There are the same economic characteristics, including the existence of two circuits: a profoundly parasitic urban economy, responding solely to the needs of the social elite, and an essentially inturned rural economy, with little money in circulation, and subject to a tributary regime. The conceptions of political life were the same, with a close association between the right of ownership and participation in public life. At the centre of this system, according to Finley, was the state, which played a decisive economic and social role. It was a state located at the centre of the 'relations of production' (in the Marxist sense of the term), since a large part of the revenues of the ruling class came from the land tax, and since its redistribution assured the 'reproduction' of the social hierarchies. It was a state placed at the centre of the economy (production and exchange) by the many functions it exercised in this sphere, imposing its own regulations and repressing or restricting the effects of the market mechanism. To such structures corresponded, according to Finley, a logic of transformation characterised by the increasing hypertrophy of the state, which would exhaust the productive capacities of Roman society and eventually cause its downfall. He concluded that the collapse of the empire brought the ancient system to an end and made way for something different.

This is one of the points at which our analysis diverges from that of Finley. There can be no doubt that the political changes resulting from the Germanic migrations were considerable. On the other hand, there was no essential change in economic, social or mental structures. The system reposed on the same principles, functioned in the same manner, and this for one simple reason: it could not do otherwise as long as the various basic structures were not destroyed. But the fracture of the state and the gradual weakening of its functions engendered multiple malfunctionings, imposed recourse to other solutions and thus determined a slow and generalised destructuring of the ancient system.

This is the point of departure. The point of arrival is characterised by the crystallisation of another set of structures, equally coherent, which would be known as 'feudal'. There were different social structures, namely the peasantry in its entirety, placed in a new relation of dependence (lordship over land and the *seigneurie banale*), and an aristocracy whose hegemony reposed on different bases. There were different economic structures, dominated by the birth of the market, the new town/country articulation and the now overwhelming predominance of small-scale family production. There were new political structures: the essential feature was not the fief, nor even the fragmentation of power, but the exercise of a direct power by the aristocracy over the producers as a body. Lastly, there were new ideological presentations: the notion of the three orders and, more precisely, the version of Odilo. Of course, everything did not happen at once. Before crystallising into a new whole or a new system, each of these structures, in a greater or lesser degree of isolation, travelled a long road within the ancient system.

Our second proposition is that in the transition from one system to another, the dominant trends were slow and gradual processes. They took place over the long term (five hundred years), and had cumulative effects, which made them difficult to reverse, despite occasional blockages, even brief backwards steps. They affected the state, the economy, religious life and social structures alike. They simultaneously encompassed the phenomena of the disintegration of the ancient order and the phenomena of its reconstitution. Lastly, they revealed many reciprocal solidarities. We need therefore to construct a rigorous typology and, above all, examine their inter-connections. We will confine ourselves here to a few illustrations.

The most active process in the destructuring of the ancient system was probably the weakening of the functions of the state (given the central role it had played). It is as if the logic revealed by Finley was reversed, atrophy succeeding hypertrophy. The state was weakened because the roots which it had plunged deep into the countryside were cut; the sap (the tax) no longer rose. The various expedients designed to revitalise it (notably the conquests) were of limited duration and impact. Other processes followed directly from it: the withering of the town where the old bureaucracy rapidly disintegrated, the decline of long distance trade through the contraction of urban demand, and the general slowing-down of trade because the circulation of money was no longer sustained by the distribution of coins to functionaries or soldiers. The decline of the state was thus a determining factor in the general ruralisation of society. But it also had consequences in many other spheres. The progress of vassalage and immunity, and the strengthening grip of the clerical apparatus, from the diocese to the rural parish, were all responses to the need to find new ways of structuring men. The organisation of the large Carolingian estate was also a response to this political context and to its commercial implications. In many respects, the political seems thus to have made the running. The state, having been the keystone of the ancient system, still, through its own decline, governed the destructuring of the old order, a destructuring which followed a vertical path from the top downwards.

Conversely, the processes of reconstitution emerged within the lower levels of the social edifice. The most obvious and probably the most active were the rise of small-scale family production and agrarian growth, clearly interrelated. They were also linked, it should be recalled, to the decline of the power of the state. The link was direct, to the extent that, by macro-economic regulation, the slackening of the fiscal vice was a factor for rural growth. But it also operated by means of numerous mediations which deserve closer examination. For example, the strengthening of the conjugal unit was, on the one hand, connected to the progress of the power of the clergy, and on the other favoured the cohesion of the small unit of domestic production, and thus became a factor in agrarian growth, from which, in its turn, it drew sustenance. On a more general level, the Christianisation of the countryside can be seen as one of the long-term processes which contributed to the global transformation of society.[2] The major impulsions for this came from above, from the ruling strata of society; they were not unconnected to the crisis of the state. But its effects went beyond a simple structuring of the faithful; it played a role in the evolution of social mentalities, engendered new needs, tended to remove the moral frontier separating the free man from the slave, and gave birth to the notion of a 'Christian people', thus accelerating social change. For these reasons, Christianisation was a factor both in the promotion of the peasantry and in agrarian growth. But for the completion of this process, the mass mobilisation realised in the 'Peace of God', and consequently the feudal revolution, would be incomprehensible.

The growth of economic forces thus first found fertile ground in the decomposing of the ancient system; in its turn, it acted on it by encouraging certain of its specific processes. It showed up the archaism of slavery; it gave vigour to the peasant communities, thus emphasising the weakness of the political structures; it gradually compelled the ruling class to expect less of the state and seek more from local economic resources; on the plane of ideas, lastly, it valorised the image of the producer.

In other words, there was no simple juxtaposition of particular processes of disintegration and reconstitution. Between the one and the other, the dialectical relations were constant and rendered irreversible what we will call the global process of transformation leading from the ancient system to the feudal system. It was a revolutionary process, in the true meaning of the word, since it tended to destroy the ancient system within which it had developed, and prepare for the emergence of a new system. Of this global process we should note two characteristics which deserve a lengthier discussion than the few remarks which follow.

In the first place, if, in the dynamic of this process, the interaction between the old and the new remained constant, the role of factors of the ancient type (notably the weakening of the state) gradually diminished to the benefit of factors of a new type; on the one hand, there was erosion, on the other, an accumulation of new elements. This may well explain why agrarian growth was extremely slow to begin with, whereas its progress then speeded up, before eventually destabilising the system as whole.

One illustration of the complex articulation between the ancient and the new is to be found in the monetary developments which affected Frankish society from the fifth to the tenth centuries, money being, as we know, one of the most sensitive indicators of the condition of a society. Initially, the Roman monetary system was retained, its gold coins meeting the needs of urban life and a long distance luxury trade. Two types of malfunction were soon apparent, consequences of the malfunctioning of the state: the end of the state monopoly and the gradual disappearance of the gold coinage, a process which was complete by the beginning of the eighth century. In parallel, the first elements of a monetary restructuring appeared with the revival of the minting of silver coins and the appearance of the *denier*, appropriate to exchanges of low value (around 625–30). The Carolingian period then expressed the maximum tension (in this as in other spheres) between the old and the new: the public character of money was restored at the expense of private mints, but it was on the basis of a silver mono-metallism which responded to the needs of a new economic climate, dominated by, precisely, agrarian growth. The circulation of silver, even though it remained small-scale, drew strength from this growth and facilitated it. The final stage was reached when the definitive political break-up of the Carolingian world allowed the emergence of local mints and, by the same title, the deep penetration of the monetary tool into the rural fabric, with the consequences we know. It is quite possible to add a dash of anthropology to this schema, with regard to the relationship between hoarding and 'primitive' attitudes towards precious metal. But the crucial fact was surely a monetary development which took place within the context of the transition from one economic system to another and participated directly in the global process; as also the increasing pressure of economic needs, and the fact that the attempt of the state to regain control of the monetary reins liberated new forces and led to its total dispossession.

A second characteristic of the global process is this: there is no justification for claiming that it was dominated by the primacy of any specific 'instance' (economic, social, political or ideological). A crude materialism, determined at all costs to give priority to the economic factor, is here as naive and dangerous as the speculative idealism for which only mentalities count. Just as the major sets of structures (or social systems) inextricably intermingled the alleged 'instances' (on which an illusory autonomy is too often conferred), so the global process which leads from the one to the other sweeps along all elements indifferently. The dialectic between the ancient and the new did not take place within superimposed and watertight strata; it developed vertically through all levels of society. At the very most one observes, on the basis of a careful examination of the various specific processes, that a particular factor assumed, at a given moment in the global process, a particularly active role. Thus at the beginning, the crisis of the state, with its many immediate consequences, manifestly made the running; then the economic, from the eighth century, seems to have taken up the baton; lastly, the ideological was, at the end of the period, placed in a decisive position to the extent that it underpinned the feudal revolution itself. This is surely simply the specific effect of a more general phenomenon: the different time-scales within the historical process. A certain precipitateness in the political domain, a slower rate of change in the economy, the immense inertia, lastly, of social mentalities. This explains the interminable length of the process of the birth of the feudal system. The transformation or revolution did not involve only the bringing into being of economic and social conditions. That the ancient order lasted so long was perhaps because of the power of the slave-owning mentality, nothing being more difficult than the eradication of social prejudice. However that may be, the problematic suggested here, far from closing the analysis, opens wide the windows on the search for the dislocations which were able to appear between the various orders of phenomena or processes, thereby constituting so many points of blockage in the global process.

After structure and process, the third essential concept is that of rupture. Nothing could in practice be more erroneous than the notion of an imperceptible transition from the ancient to the feudal world, under the influence of the various processes described above; nor was Frankish society a hybrid society, half ancient, half feudal, whose old and new elements we need to assess. All its structures attach it to the model of ancient societies, That said, the slow maturing which took place within it culminated in ruptures or, more precisely, a global rupture. In the Mâconnais, twenty to twenty-five years sufficed to transform the social landscape from top to bottom. This, perhaps, was the specificity of the revolution of the year 1000: it was all the more rapid and all the more complete in that it had been so long maturing. We should note, in any case, its principal features. Firstly, it appeared when society, under the influence of multiple disequilibriums of an economic, social and political nature, could no longer be governed as in the past and had sunk into anarchy (the violence of the men of war). Secondly, the rupture affected every sphere, it crystallised into a new set or system all those elements which had previously emerged, relating to the status of men and land just as much as to the distribution of power, economic mechanisms and social representations.

It will further be noted that the notion of rupture does not apply only to the political sphere. In the economic field, too, it appears that trade and the market took off with dramatic suddeness in the decade 970–80, promoted by the slow social and economic maturing of the countryside, but till then checked by the persistence of ancient structures (slavery and the unilateral relationship between town and country).

Conceptual repercussions

Such a problematic has conceptual repercussions or implications which it is preferable to mention explicitly even though these implications have already become apparent on a number of occasions. We will note only the two main ones.

What are these 'sets of structures' or 'social systems' (ancient and feudal)? This is a question which it is impossible to avoid. Without a clear and workable concept for the point of departure and the point of arrival, the study of the progress from the one to the other (the global process and the rupture) is compromised and can give rise to only a rather disjointed erudition.

Historical materialism has long provided an answer to this question: it sees them as 'modes of production'. Is this a workable concept in this instance? Its evident value is to emphasise the presence at the heart of these systems of specific relations of exploitation, in the one case, slavery, in the other, the seigneurie. On this point, there can be not a shadow of doubt. The most fundamental significance of the revolution of the year 1000 was certainly located at this level. It was primarily a social and mental transformation: a historic change, after centuries of slavery, in the manner of profiting from the labour of others, and the establishment of a relation of exploitation on which European societies would be based for not far short of another thousand years. This is by no means negligible, especially if one is willing to accept that people's labour, in all its aspects, is central to their history. I therefore see no serious grounds for consigning this concept to the scrap-heap. The real problem is rather the function which has been assigned to it and the use made of it by traditional Marxism.

On this last point, a radical revision is necessary. The claim to make it into an all-embracing concept cannot be justified. To attempt to explain the principal changes operating at the heart of a given society wholly in terms of the mode of production, its contradictions and the class struggle which was their expression is a terribly reductionist approach. It quickly assumes a theological and dogmatic character. Traditional Marxism has got bogged down in this approach; obsessed by the relation of production and by a few sentences of Marx and Engels, it has persisted in locating the decisive change in the appearance of the Roman colonate, expunging every other social reality, ignoring the persistence of an essential slavery and the global continuity of ancient structures, ignoring, ultimately, the feudal revolution itself. The error is of the same type as that which, with regard to contemporary societies, consists of confusing nationalisation or state control of the economy with socialism. It is the perverse result of putting ideology before reason.

The concept of social system is taken here in a wider sense. It encompasses the mode of production (which is a foundation of the system) but goes beyond it. It expresses the coherence of a set of structures over and above the simple relation of exploitation. Thus, when Finley speaks of the 'ancient system', he relates it to slavery, certainly, but he does not forget that the 'relations of production' cannot be reduced to the master/slave confrontation; he does not ignore the structuring role of the state (especially in the exploitation of the free peasantry by fiscal means), or the existence of an economy which functions in its own way. In the historical process, the master/slave contradiction is not the only one to matter; it may be relegated to the background by the logic of the social system taken as a whole. This is the case when Finley discusses the development of the Late Empire, a development dominated by the growing hypertrophy of the state. In so doing, Finley inaugurated (by the same title as Witold Kula for a different historical period)[3] a profound regeneration of historical materialism.[4]

Lastly, does the notion of social system bear a family relationship to that of 'world economy'? Fernand Braudel has been the most influential and creative French historian of the second half of the twentieth century (a role reserved for Marc Bloch in the first half). Braudel was obsessed by the need for broad conceptualisation. He offered a specific response by formulating the concept of world economy and applying it to vast historical groupings, strongly structured and hierarchised, with their centre, their concentric zones and their peripheries.[5] His approach was clearly different from that proposed here; it emphasised the economic to the detriment of the social, the sphere of exchange to the detriment of production; it claimed to be an alternative to the globalising demands of Marxism. All of which matters less than the fact that its contribution is of immense importance. The notion of social system must draw freely on it. Braudel threw light on one of its hidden faces. The social system is not only a coherent set of structures, it has a projection in space, frontiers, a centre, concentric zones; it forms an organic whole at the heart of which an imbalance of trade plays a major role.

To understand the transition from ancient to feudal society, it is necessary to integrate this dimension. The micro-historical approach adopted in this study might appear to have distanced me from such a perspective. It is time to turn to it, if only in a few words. The ancient system was a world economy dominated first by Rome, then by Constantinople. Merovingian Gaul was surely only a periphery on the way to being detached from a whole whose impulsions still came from the shores of the Bosporus. The meagre traffic which animated the port of Mâcon was only a final ramification of a long distance trade, the principal currents of which originated in the eastern Mediterranean. The destructuring of the ancient system in the West was also assisted, therefore, by the loosening of the grip of the centre on the periphery, by the growing autonomy of Latin Christianity on all fronts, religious, monetary and commercial, political. The loosening was uneven as a function of degrees of proximity or remoteness and, above all, of the unequal degree to which ancient structures had become entrenched in different places. It was therefore inconceivable that the global process of disintegration/reintegration discussed above would assume a uniform character. The unevenness of the process in space is even necessarily the rule. On the geographical plane, we should thus look for differences in rates of progress and points of blockage, one of the best indicators being provided by the very variable degree of dissociation of the state structures of Italy and England. Such an approach might lead to the posing in new terms of the comparative study of the evolution of the societies within the two Christendoms. However that may be, the feudal revolution also gave birth to a feudal 'world economy', rapidly achieving a dominant position by the end of the eleventh century.

The second question concerns the dynamic of social systems. To the extent that the system embodies a 'mode of production', its dynamic owes much to it. Thus the ultimate backdrop to the transition from ancient to feudal society had its roots in the crisis of slavery, that is in the impossibility, by the Late Empire, of maintaining servile exploitation in its crudest forms. This is perhaps a point in the work of Finley which has been underestimated. But this subterranean contradiction did not act directly on the political or social conjuncture. It was mediated by all the other elements of the social system. No theoretical essay forged on the basis of a mythical vision of the class struggle can get round this fact. The slaves did not overthrow the ancient system. Their class struggle consisted primarily of gradually consolidating their social promotion and integrating themselves into the 'Christian people'. Conversely, the free peasantry did not have as its goal the overthrow of the ancient order, but its dynamism made a major contribution to its decline. The same was true of the aristocracy when it was party to the dismantling of the state.

In other words, the notion of social system in no way implies a structural vision closed in on itself, a sort of machine, whose gears are invisible except when they wear out or corrode over time. It was from the action of the social forces that the whole dynamic surely came. But this action presented forms and took paths which were often unexpected. The key to reading the social system, by revealing the existence of objective processes, makes it possible to understand better the impact and the limitations of the pressure exercised by social forces. They did not determine the nature of the process (it was dictated by the structure itself), but they checked or accelerated its course. Their action took place within the framework which was imposed on them and from which they were unable to free themselves; hence the sometimes paradoxical results.

The paradox, in the event, was that the feudal revolution drew strength from the movement of the peasantry: from its rise in the long term, from its direct intervention in the final phase. So, in effect, this class helped to place in the saddle those who were to dominate and exploit it for centuries, within the context of the seigneurie. But perhaps this is not the only way we should look at it. We should perhaps not regard as negligible the achievement by the peasants of a new socio-economic status which guaranteed them, through tenure, the stability of their rights to land, and which made of them quite distinct economic agents, endowed with a real autonomy in production and trade. The feudal revolution inaugurated the true age of the peasantry. Certainly, like other revolutions, it had an oppressive face, but initially it was a liberation.

Notes

1 François Dosse, *L'Histoire en miettes. Des 'Annales' à la 'nouvelle histoire'*, Paris, 1987.
2 Not only Christianisation properly speaking, but also the slow emergence of a more personal religion, in correlation with the promotion, in the social and economic order, of the restricted family group.
3 Kula, *An Economic Theory of the Feudal System.*
4 The recent synthesis (albeit highly intelligent and stimulating) attempted by Chris Wickham seems to me to err by an ambiguity at this level. On the one hand, he adopts as his starting point the 'ancient system' of Finley (with everything that implies from the conceptual point of view), on the other, he subsequently argues only in terms of the relations of production (forgetting en route the global system) in his attempt to discover at what moment the new assumed greater importance than the ancient, wholly in the tradition of 'traditional' Marxism. I, for my part, see this as a flaw in Wickham's conceptual coherence, as if he had got stuck in mid-stream (Wickham, 'The other transition'). His very use of the concept of 'transition' demands critical comment (it is in contradiction to the very marked coherence of the ancient system

which he takes as his starting point).
5 F. Braudel, *Civilisation matérielle, Economic et capitalisme, XVe–XVIIIe siècle*, vol. 3, *Le Temps du Monde*, Paris, 1979, pp. 12–55.

Appendix: The seven families of the *ager* of Merzé

Bold type indicates the principal persons in the years 980–1000

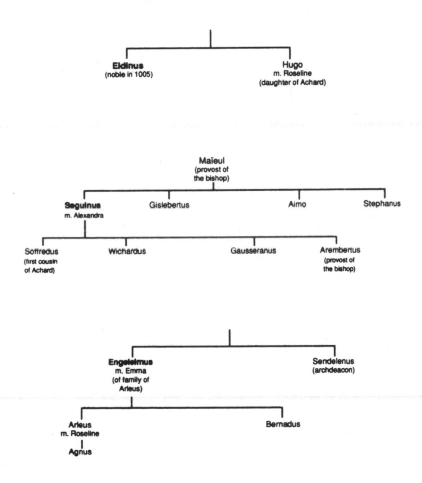

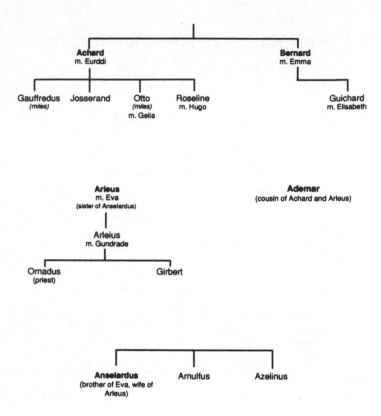

Select index